THE SPIRIT AND THE BRIDE

Also by Dom Anscar Vonier
Published by Assumption Press

The Human Soul and its Relations with Other Spirits

The Personality of Christ

A Key to the Doctrine of the Eucharist

The Christian Mind

The Divine Motherhood

The Life of the World to Come

The Art of Christ: Retreat Conferences

The Angels

Death and Judgement

The New and Eternal Covenant

Christ the King of Glory

Christianus

The Victory of Christ

The People of God

Sketches and Studies in Theology

THE SPIRIT
AND THE BRIDE

DOM ANSCAR VONIER

ASSUMPTION PRESS

2013

✠ Nihil Obstat.
Innocentius Apap, S.Th.M., O.P.,
Censor Deputatus.

✠ Imprimatur.
Joseph Butt,
Vicarius Generalis.

Westminster
September 17, 1935

The *Nihil Obstat* and *Imprimatur* are official declarations
that a book or pamphlet is free of doctrinal or moral error.
No implication is contained therein that those who have
granted the *Nihil Obstat* and the *Imprimatur* agree
with the content, opinions or statements expressed.

This book was originally published in 1935
by Burns, Oates, and Washbourne.

Cover image: *Pentecôte*, Jean II Restout, 1732

CONTENTS

✠

FOREWORD

MANY FRIENDS HAVE REPEATEDLY ASKED ME TO WRITE a book on the Holy Ghost. A very short period of thought on the subject has convinced me of the futility of treating of the Holy Ghost without at the same time speaking of the Church; it would be tantamount to giving a theological exposition on the Second Person of the Trinity without mentioning the Incarnation. Hence the double name under which this book goes forth. Obviously the passage in the last chapter of St. John's Apocalypse has suggested the title: "And the Spirit and the Bride say: Come" (Rev 22:17). The Spirit is the Holy Ghost and the Bride is the Church.

Perhaps more than one reader will complain that he does not find in this book the usual clear descriptions of the marks of the Church, oneness, holiness, catholicity, apostolicity. It has been the writer's chief effort to present the Church as the manifest work of the Holy Ghost, nay, even as the evidence of the Holy Ghost's presence. He does not think that having approached the Church's theology from this angle he has neglected any of the essential aspects that belong to an orthodox treatise *de Ecclesia*, "about the Church," though the matter may have a less systematic arrangement.

I have noticed with a feeling of pain how several recent books by Catholic writers of fame make a distinction that is a surrender to Protestant feeling between the ideal Church and the real Church. Being themselves very orthodox Catholics the writers in question abound, of course, in their encomiums of the beauty of the Church conceived ideally. But after that they seem to gloat on the Church's human infirmities, piling it on and letting the Protestant have it his own way with his century-old fault-finding. Different, indeed, was the mentality of the Vatican Council which considered the Church in her actuality to be a *testimonium irrefragibile*, a "witness that cannot be gainsaid," of her divine mission:

> The Church, through herself, on account of her admirable extension (*propagationem*), her exceeding sanctity (*eximiam sanctitatem*), her inexhaustible stability, is a great and everlasting motive of credibility and a witness to her divine mission that cannot be gainsaid (*Vatican I*, sess. III, cap. 3, 7).

The Council means, of course, the actual living Church, not an ideal, or a mere system of the means of sanctification. To say the least, it is very bad taste on the part of a Catholic to represent Catholicism as a divine religion and to speak of Catholics as having been the world's worst sinners. Such flippancy ought not to be tolerated any longer. The *eximia sanctitas*, "exceptional holiness," which the last of the General Councils perceived in the Church is the true portrait of what exists. In this book I have followed the guidance of the greatest Church assembly of modern times.

In any literature on the Church there occurs a difficulty which had better be met at once in this Foreword.

The point at issue is what can be denominated hypostatizing of the Church, that is to say the practice of speaking of her as of a person. She is called the Bride, to confine ourselves to the title of the book. Now such hypostatizings are familiar to human literature and to popular imagination. Countries are given personal names; they are even loved as beautiful figures, chiefly of the female gender. Instances are at hand, but need not be quoted. Is this process of hypostatizing more justified, has it a truer basis than is the case with national affection and racial idealism? It is, of course, evident that with regard to the Church the idealization took place long before it existed in national sentiment: it is as old as Christianity. But whatever may be the psychological explanation of this process in ordinary human life, it is certain that there is in the Church an element which is unique and cannot be found in nature. The Spirit of God, a divine Person, is to the scattered Christian souls of all times and all climes a bond of life and union that is not thinkable elsewhere. The presence of that Spirit amongst the faithful, as I hope to show in this book, is more than the separate sanctification of many thousands, nay, many millions, of individual souls. There is the mystery of the one life: nature has nothing analogous. To give the Church the name of Bride is more than literature. It is a theological necessity. Without such a name or its equivalent we could never know the true relationship between the Church and Christ, we could not express the special operation of the Spirit who came down at Pentecost.

Anscar Vonier, O.S.B., *Abbot.*
Buckfast, Pentecost, 1935

✠ 1 ✠

THE BURDEN OF THE CHURCH

WHEN CATHOLICS PROFESS THAT THEY ARE A CHURCH, they assume a very heavy responsibility. It is as if a group of men came together and constituted themselves into a well-defined society with an unmistakable nomenclature and then proceeded to proclaim to the world at large that they were an invincible set of heroes whose corporate existence no power on earth could terminate. In protesting that they are a Church, Catholics are committing themselves to a pretension not less rash, nay, immensely more daring. They say to all men who are willing to listen, and even shout it into the ears of those who are unwilling, that they are a divinely constituted society which is quite proof against any dissolving agency, so that for endless aeons there never will be a hostile power strong enough to pull it down or to sap its foundations.

They go even further and pretend that this society of theirs gives at all times such signs of its excellence that its divine character becomes manifest. To do this, as we have said, is to assume an appalling responsibility. It is to invite trouble, to ask for hostility, to provoke criticism of the bitterest kind and to set all the rest of humanity on a course of merciless fault-finding. Who would not, with a scream of exultation, hold up before all eyes the sins of a society that proclaims itself divine? If Christians had never embarked on this incredible claim to be a divinely created society, how much more comfortable things would have been! Their shortcomings, far from scandalizing the world, would have brought forth from men's hearts the balm of human sympathy; they would have been treated with utmost indulgence. After all, to sin is only human, even in the case of those who have faith in a God Incarnate. "But," says the world, "if you maintain amongst us the intolerable claim that you are a Church, a society of elect spirits, a corporate power with a right to dictate in the matters of the soul and in the concerns of the conscience, an indestructible association of men with a divine call, then be ready to suffer the consequences of so provocative a pose. Every one of your weaknesses, every sin committed by you, we shall contemplate with pleasure; we shall dance with joy over your moral frailties, because the clay feet of the idol will have revealed themselves."

Let us consider how easy would be the lot of Christians if every one of them were an isolated mystic, a budding idealist following an entirely solitary road. For the Christian who has no brethren in Christ except in the vaguest sense, the scandal of the Cross is greatly reduced; Christ in Himself may be all that the most imaginative Christian can desire. His divinity will create no real objections. His miracles will be taken on their own merits, His resurrection and ascension will not arouse an animus in men, because, after all, if it so happened, why not leave it at that? The Christian, without anyone either on his right hand or his left to be connected with him, will make his best of such a Christ. He may rise to high loyalties towards Him or he may disappoint Him most miserably. He may do things in turn. The contests of the spirit, the struggle between Satan and Christ in that soul will not be a concern to alarm the world, though it may be of interest. To such Christians would be applicable the word which Christ Himself spoke of His brethren, His cousins in the flesh: "The world cannot hate you" (John 7:7). Hatred begins there where power or the pretension to power begins: "But me it hateth, because I give testimony of it, that the works thereof are evil" (John 7:7). Let there be a group of men to whom the same truths concerning Christ are a bond of unity, are as the breath of life, then the benevolent tolerance of the outsider will suddenly become fierce enmity. It is certain that at no time, even in the days of Nero, would Christians have been persecuted if they had not been dreaded, if they had not stood in the way of someone's ambition or folly, if, above all, they had not been suspected of being a band of conspirators, a union of sinister forces. It was not clear at all times to the enemies of Christianity to what degree Christians were constituting one compact spiritual society; but the adversaries of the Christian name knew enough to make them uneasy; they realized that they had to do with an organized force. Persecutions of all times and of every scale of severity were directed against a power, not against the individual and dispersed votaries of an impalpable faith.

But this obstinate determination of Catholics to proclaim themselves to be a Church, a supernatural state, has elicited something worse than the furies of the persecutor; it has created the great scandal. The scandal comes, of course, from the obvious fact that the self-styled divine society is anything but divine in its manifest life and its visible works. For let us bear in mind that the Christian attributes to his Church a sort of divinity which he would never dare to arrogate to himself; the Church in his eyes possesses, actually and literally, immense spiritual prerogatives of which he himself is merely the beneficiary. His Church is to him an absolute reality, though he himself may be imperfect and incomplete in grace, with endless variations in the degrees of his fervor. Now through this assumption the case of Catholicism is, as we have said already, most unfavorable, for it produces the great scandal: "It must needs be that scandals come" (Matt 18:7).

"Where is that godlike society?" asks the infidel. "Is it not the very reason of my rebellion," says the heretic, "that the so-called divine Church is full of all abominations?" Holy men and women there have been in the Church; even a selfish and corrupt world will speak kindly of them and see the romance of their existence; in fact it is quite in keeping with all we know of our own civilization that the most unlikely people will believe in the sanctity of some individual disciple of Christ. But no one will be found, in these days, outside Catholicism, who will speak well of the Church. If Christians have been good individually, as a Church they have failed miserably. Such is the modern verdict.

There is, moreover, another difficulty incurred by those Christians who obstinately cling to the notion of a society, which free discipleship with Christ would avoid. He who wants a Church asks for dissensions: "For there must be also heresies: that they also, who are approved may be made manifest" (1 Cor 11:19). How much easier would it be to let every man follow the spirit in his own way, abound in his own sense, take and leave as much of the mystery of Christ as is good for his own contentment. Why exact oneness and uniformity of belief, that *conditio sine qua non,* "necessary condition," of the Church idea? Would not the course of Christianity have been infinitely more peaceful had there not been the obsession for dogmatic supremacy? Was the uniformity of belief worth all that anguish of spirit, all that disappointment of soul, which those have suffered on whom oneness of faith has been pressed as a good to be prized above all goods? Would not charity have gained immensely, or more truly, not have suffered such enormous breaches, had there been none of that doctrinal absolutism which is the first fatal result of the Church pretence? Moreover, there is the almost insurmountable peril of dissension that comes from men of all races and civilizations being forced to dwell in one house of faith. Is such leveling of the finest qualities of human originality really worth the trouble? Are not those much wiser who give race and blood a primary place, who graft the belief in Christ on nationhood, who never dream of anything vaster than a national church, as anything vaster is bound to snap? Why keep warring races within the bosom of the same Spiritual mother, the Church? Is it not evident that a tribe or a nation shepherded by a benign temporal prince would be a most edifying portion of Christ's flock if left to pursue the faith in its own way, without thought of what other Christians across the political frontier I may fancy?

A further and supreme disadvantage of the Church obedience, in the eyes of many, is the binding and imprisoning of the Spirit. There must surely be, it is said, a diminution of the action of the Spirit within the walls of the city of the Church. "The Spirit breatheth where he will" (John 3:8), saith Christ. A circumscribed faith, an iron discipline, are fetters, not wings. Mystics will either desert the Church or, if they have to remain within it, their lives will have hardly anything in common with the Catholicism of the ordinary believer, or they will be long, drawn-out martyrdoms of the soul. The freedom of the Spirit is bound to assert itself; if mountains of human legislation were piled upon it to keep it under, it would one day shake off the mass and liberate itself. Has not the Church mania rendered Catholics intellectually impossible? Would they not themselves, were they quite honest, welcome more elasticity in the dogmatic formulas which are the granite blocks that form the defense of the Church? Has not many a thinker and a mystic heaved a groan of relief when ultimately, after long struggles, he has left the Church, saying: *Liberavi animam meam,* "I have freed my soul"? Certainly, if Christianity had been left to that primitive simplicity when every man finds Christ in his own way, goes to Christ in his own grace, fits Christ into his own scheme of thought, much spiritual misery would never have been known.

This despair of the Church's power to justify herself would be an excusable sentiment, but for that very fact of truly infinite magnitude which makes all the difference between human associations and that one association of which we speak. It is true that all history is there and all experience is there to bring it home to us that if individual goodness is difficult, corporate goodness is well-nigh impossible, at least for any length of time. Men will soon go their own ways, even in their ideals. Shepherds are few, and without them the sheep are soon scattered. But is not this Catholicism, to believe that what is not possible to the human race is possible to a power that transcends the race, to a power of unification that comes from above, that descends from heaven—the Spirit of God, the Holy Ghost? Unless we started with the faith that it is through the Holy Ghost that the Church is vivified and unified, we should indeed make of the Church ideal an extravagant claim and an intolerable burden; a Church is thinkable only in the hypothesis of the Spirit of God dwelling in many hearts, uniting them, purifying them and constantly raising them above their individual sinfulness and their natural selfishness.

Catholicism considers the Holy Ghost to be the unceasing power of compensation inside the Church, equalizing, out of the depth of His own charity, all the inequalities of individual Christian lives.

Truly, without such an element of compensation the human deficits would be too great for a Church to avoid being broken as a spiritual concern. Any amount of panicky sentiments for the future of the Church would be justified unless we had the assurance that the Church lives, not by herself, but through the Spirit:

> But you are not in the flesh, but in the spirit, if so be that the Spirit of God dwell in you. Now if any man have not the Spirit of Christ, he is none of His (Rom 8:9).

Christ Himself protests His confidence in the Spirit for the success of His own work. All the hatred of the world will come to naught, all the powers of darkness will be put to shame because there is the Spirit:

> If I had not done among them the works that no other man hath done, they would not have sin: but now they have both seen and hated both me and my Father. But that the word may be fulfilled, which is written in their law: They hated me without cause. But when the Paraclete cometh, whom I will send you from the Father, the Spirit of truth, who proceedeth from the Father, he shall give testimony of me. And you shall give testimony, because you are with me from the beginning (John 15:24-27).

Truly the Spirit who came ought to give courage to all of us, since His coming reassured the heart of even the Son of God when He walked towards His cross and to His death.

The Catholic in his thoughts on the Church must necessarily adopt an aprioristic attitude. This is his faith; so if anything is said against the Church in the past he will answer quite naturally that nothing has happened that could possibly drive out the Holy Ghost from the Church at any time. Which circumstance is, of course, the supreme fact that matters. Of the present-day Church and of the future, the Catholic not only augurs well, but pronounces with absolute certainty that the Spirit is with her, the Spirit will be with her, and this by definition, for it is the Church's definition to be a society unceasingly inhabited by the Holy Ghost, who dwells in her, not as in a ruin, but as in a temple:

> Know you not that your members are the temple of the Holy Ghost, who is in you, whom you have from God: and you are not your own (1 Cor 6:19)?

✠ 2 ✠

THE COMING OF THE SPIRIT

IT IS THE CHRISTIAN'S HAPPY POSITION TO BE AT ALL times in immediate contact with the Spirit; he has the Spirit in himself and wherever he looks within the immense precincts of the Church he sees the Spirit, and by Spirit we mean of course, the Holy Ghost, the Third Person of the Blessed Trinity. The Church is the home of the Spirit and there is nothing so near, nothing so present on this earth as the Spirit is near and present. The Spirit is invisible, but this does not mean that the Spirit is not manifest. For this is the New Testament characteristic of the Spirit, that He is a most evident power, not a hidden, imperceptible force. Since the ascension, the Spirit, in exact New Testament thought, is a more manifest presence amongst men than is the presence of the Word Incarnate, the Son of God, the Second Person of the Trinity. Of Christ it is said that He is hidden in the glory of heaven:

> Whom the heaven indeed must receive, until the times of
> the restitution of all things, which God hath spoken by the

mouth of his holy prophets, from the beginning of the world (Acts 3:21).

If He is present in the Church it is in the abysmal hiddenness of the Sacrament. Of the Spirit it is said, on the contrary, that He is shown forth, that He is felt like a mighty wind, that He is seen as a burning fire, that He is everything except a hidden God. We are, perhaps, little accustomed to look upon the Spirit as upon the manifestation of God and His Christ amongst men; we are more inclined to establish this difference between the coming of Christ and the coming of the Spirit, that the first is manifest whilst the second is hidden. Such is not original Christian thinking. According to apostolic language it is Christ who hides after He accomplished His work here on earth and it is the Spirit who is made manifest. The Spirit is the true theophany after Christ's ascension till the Lord returns again from heaven in the glory of the Father.

The coming of the Spirit in the New Testament is a most manifest phenomenon; He, Himself, in His own Person does the manifesting, He is not dispatching angels to warn men that He has come. When the Second Person of the Trinity was born in Bethlehem it was not He but angels who announced the great news that Christ the Lord had been born: the Child never spoke. A star guided worshippers to the house where there dwelt the Mother and the Babe. Angels, again, brought the message of Christ's resurrection. With the one exception of the moment of the transfiguration, the Son of God did not show Himself in His power during His life on earth, His works were His testimony. Different is the coming of the Spirit. He arrives with glory, with power; there is no kind of economy in the signs of His presence. Nor is it a progressive unveiling, a concealment from men to be followed by partial revelation. On the contrary, the advent of the Spirit is as complete at the first Pentecost as will be the coming of the Son of God in the glory of the Father at the end of the world. We may truly say that the first coming of the Son and of the Spirit are opposite in their plans. The Spirit at once shows His full measure of presence, whilst the Son begins with the smallest measure; the fullness of manifestation is not to be reached till the day on which He will come with power and majesty at the end of the world.

It is on account of this full measure of presence since Pentecost that the kingdom of God is truly said to be with us on this earth, because the Spirit abides with us in the fullness of His divinity, not with a transient and provisional economy; the Spirit will never be more with man than He is today, simply because He is now with man in the fullest degree. The Spirit came at Pentecost, not as a mere seed, not as one who intends to reveal Himself progressively, but as the fulfillment of all the promises that had been made, as the crowning of all the preceding work, as the triumph that ends a long warfare. The coming of the Spirit in that hour was a consummation, in the sense that through this event endless centuries of preparation received their explanation and their accomplishment.

No one ever came with such completeness as did the Spirit; no one ever arrived with such a resolve to abide for ever as was the manner of the Paraclete. For it is in the very nature of His coming that He should abide. It was not His will to come in order to do a work and then go back after its accomplishment, His advent was not intended to prepare for a further dispensation. He came finally, totally, permanently, as the kingdom of God of which there shall be no end. He is the Spirit of promise, not because He promises a higher dispensation to follow His presence, but because He is the realization of all the promises that went before: He is the pledge of our inheritance, because through Him we have become the heirs of all that God had prepared for the elect from the beginning.

The manner of the coming of the Spirit cannot be described otherwise than in the identical words of the sacred text:

> And when the days of the Pentecost were accomplished, they were all together in one place. And suddenly there came a sound from heaven, as of a mighty wind coming: and it filled the whole house where they were sitting. And there appeared to them parted tongues, as it were of fire: and it sat upon every one of them. And they were all filled with the Holy Ghost: and they began to speak with diverse tongues, according as the Holy Ghost gave them to speak. Now there were dwelling at Jerusalem, Jews, devout men, out of every nation under heaven. And when this was noised abroad, the multitude came together and were confounded in mind, because that every man heard them speak in his own tongue. And they were all amazed and wondered, saying: Behold, are not all these that speak, Galileans? And how have we heard, every man our own tongue wherein we were born? Parthians and Medes and Elamites and inhabitants of Mesopotamia, Judea, and Cappadocia, Pontus and Asia, Phrygia and Pamphylia, Egypt and the parts of Libya about Cyrene, and strangers of Rome, Jews also and proselytes, Cretans and Arabians: we have heard them speak in our own tongues the wonderful works of God. And they were all astonished and wondered, saying one to another: what meaneth this (Acts 2:1-12)?

Nothing would be easier than to establish a comparison between this narration of the advent of the Spirit and the account of Christ's con-

ception and birth: the same inspired writer, St. Luke, is the author of
both narratives. In order to do full justice to the comparison we must
put side by side the two adorable Persons concerned, the Son of God,
whose coming is told in the first chapter of St. Luke's Gospel, and the
Third Person of the Blessed Trinity, whose entry into the life of the
Church is described in the second chapter of the Acts.

The external settings are as different as they could be. The cave
of Bethlehem and an hour of the night, with great silence everywhere; such are the well-known features of the Birth of Christ. The
angelic message and the singing of the multitude of heavenly spirits
were indeed a mighty proclamation of what had happened, but a few
shepherds only were allowed to be the witnesses of this celestial phenomenon.

The Spirit, on the contrary, chose for His coming the city of cit-
ies, Jerusalem; the busy hour of the morning, when life is at its fullest,
the great feast that brings together men from all nations. A mighty
wind, and tongues of fire are the signs of the Spirit. The whole event
is calculated to make an impression so great that the immense crowd
is swayed by it: "And they were all astonished and wondered, saying
one to another: what meaneth this?" (Acts 2:12) Another of the marvels was the spiritual ecstasy into which the Apostles were thrown;
they themselves, not heavenly spirits, spoke the "Wonderful works of
God." (Acts 2:11) There is at once a complete maturity of spiritual life;
the silence of the Child of Bethlehem is here replaced by a miraculous
prodigality of speech by men: "And they began to speak with diverse
tongues; according as the Spirit gave them to speak" (Acts 2:4).

To the ripeness of spiritual life is added at once the manly enterprise of external activity: "Peter standing up with the eleven, lifted up
his voice" (Acts 2:14). Even the mocking suggestion of the unbelievers

in that hour of overwhelming solemnity has its significance: "These men are full of new wine" (Acts 2:13). The behavior of the Apostles under the impression of the Spirit was in the highest degree sensational; their actions, in spite of themselves, were a direct challenge to normality. St. Peter admits the fact of their spiritual intoxication, but he rejects the base calumny with the simplest possible consideration; it is but the early morning: "For these are not drunk, as you suppose, seeing it is but the third hour of the day" (Acts 2:15).

We could go on for a considerable time working out the differences of the two theophanies, Christ's birth and the descent of the Holy Ghost. The more we meditate on the matter the more we realize the meaning of those words of Christ in the Gospel of St. John where He speaks of Himself as one who must go away and of the Spirit as of one who is coming:

> I tell you the truth: it is expedient to you that I go. For if I go not, the Paraclete will not come to you: but if I go, I will send him to you (John 16:7).

Peter, himself, speaks of the Holy Ghost who had come in these words: "He (God) hath poured forth this which you see and hear" (Acts 2:33). Seeing and hearing the Spirit was within the power of every man who was in Jerusalem on that day.

It may not be without profit to the reader to be reminded here of a great theological principle: the Holy Ghost Himself came on that day under all those signs which are enumerated by St. Luke, the wind, the parted tongues of fire, the power of speech, the ecstasy of the mind, which made the Apostles pour forth words over the marvels of God. Those signs were the immediate indication of the presence of the Spirit; the Holy Ghost produced them to show His advent, there was no intermediate ministry. In virtue of those signs and wonders it is as accurate, theologically, to say that the Holy Ghost *came* at the first Pentecost as it is to say that the Son of God *came* on the first Christmas night: the external forms were different, but there was no difference in the completeness and realism of the advents. The Son took unto Himself a human nature, our flesh: the Spirit uses signs and wonders. I purposely employ the present tense in the word "uses" because the sign remains as much as Christ's humanity remains, as we shall see presently.

Again we must hold that Pentecost is specifically the mystery of the Third Person of the Blessed Trinity, just as Christmas is the mystery of the Second Person of the Trinity. Neither the Father nor the Spirit took flesh when the Word was incarnated; so likewise neither the Father nor the word were signified by all that happened on the first day of Pentecost; it was exclusively the Spirit that was demonstrated. Over and over again in our theology on the Holy Ghost and His relation with the Church we must go back to the Acts of the Apostles, which are truly the *evangelium*, "gospel," of the Spirit, the Lord, and Vivifier.

I need not enter here into another very important aspect of Catholic theology through which it is maintained that all the external results in the world of nature and grace which are attributed to one divine Person are really the joint operation of the Three divine Persons. This inseparability in all operations *ad extra*, "to the exterior," of the Three Persons of the Godhead, is perfectly compatible with that other series of dogmatic facts: that it was the Son who took flesh from the Virgin Mary and the Son alone; and that it was the Spirit, the Third Person, who manifested Himself at Pentecost, and not the Two other Persons.

So for all practical purposes we speak of all that followed upon Pentecost as being the manifestations of the Spirit; and this language is accurate, for truly it is the Spirit's special privilege to manifest Himself through certain realities of the created order and above all through the sanctity of the Church. The Spirit showed Himself for the first time under the form of a dove, when Christ was baptized; it was as true an apparition of the Spirit as the Pentecostal manifestation. The dove also was the sign of the Spirit, but it was a theophany whose beneficiary was the human nature of the Son of God, not the Church, as she did not yet exist. At Pentecost, however, the Church was the beneficiary of the Spirit's outpouring, not Christ's human nature.

The one point of supreme importance is this, that we should consider the Spirit as a great manifestation of God, a declaration of a divine presence which no man can deny unless he be among those who mocked on the first Pentecost day. Visibility of the Spirit's kingdom is the great dogma which every Catholic sets out to defend. On the other hand, the finality of the advent of the Spirit is one of the pivotal truths that make Catholicism what it is; for the Catholic, the kingdom of God is already here on earth, because the Spirit will never be more manifest than He is. Substantially, the Spirit is as much with us as He will be for all eternity, though modally there may be a difference between this aeon and the glorious world to come:

I will ask the Father: and he shall give you another Paraclete, that he may abide with you forever (John 14:16).

It is, of course, possible for men to fail to see the kingdom of the Spirit in spite of its notes and signs. Not all men in Jerusalem at Pentecost gave a right explanation of what was before their eyes. This blindness of man in no wise diminishes the evidence of the Spirit's presence. It is the world's peculiar curse to be ignorant of this obvious fact just as it is the grace of the children of God to know "the Spirit of truth, whom the world cannot receive because it seeth him not, nor knoweth him. But you shall know him; because he shall abide with you and shall be in you" (John 14:17).

✠ 3 ✠

The Bride as the Sign
of the Spirit

EVEN A SUPERFICIAL READING OF THE ACCOUNT BY St. Luke of the coming of the Spirit reveals the fact that the group of men on whom the Holy Ghost descended were the principal prodigy of that day. The transformation that took place in them, the powers which they showed forth, the ecstasy in which they moved, were the overwhelming prodigy. The mighty wind and the parted tongues were signs of a passing nature; the "speaking" of the disciples was the permanent sign. It was that sign which threw the multitude into a confusion of wonderment:

> And they were all amazed and wondered saying: Behold, are not all these that speak, Galileans (Acts 2:7)?

This spiritual ecstasy, with its accompanying power of speech, must have gone on for hours, until the whole town was made aware of it; thousands of men and women must have come into contact with those holy ones in that state of spiritual delirium. The sacred historian gives us, of course, only the summary of the talk that filled Jerusalem:

> How have we heard, every man our own tongue wherein we were born? … we have heard them speak in our own tongues the wonderful works of God (Acts 2:8, 11).

These utterances the writer puts on the lips of Parthians and Medes, of Mesopotamians and Judeans, in fact, of men "out of every nation under heaven." That body of Christians was the real and permanent sign of the coming of the Spirit. To the external symbol of wind and parted tongues of fire was added the more astonishing sign of human beings thus taken out of themselves and made an object of amazement to all men.

This leads us to a consideration of paramount importance in the doctrine of the Spirit, namely, that the Spirit is truly said to have come because He has made use of created signs to show His advent and His presence. Now the principal created sign is that entirely transformed group of human beings, the hundred and twenty persons who had gone to the upper room with Peter and John, James and Andrew, Philip and Thomas, Bartholomew and Matthew, James of Alpheus and Simon Zelotes and Jude the brother of James, with the women and with Mary the Mother of Jesus and His brethren; they were the Church, and they were made by the Spirit the external sign of His having come for ever.

The Church, then, through the very laws of her birth has the position of a sign, of a *signum*. As Jesus in His infancy was declared to be a *signum*, a "sign," so the Church was born through this, that in her own body she manifested to all men that the Spirit of promise had come. This is indeed the guiding idea in the sweet matter of the Spirit and the Bride, of the Holy Ghost and the Church, that the Church from the very beginning, through her very constitution, through all the life that is in her, proclaims to the world that the Spirit of promise has been sent. The Church is as truly the symbol of the Spirit as was the dove at Christ's baptism, and through this fact the spirituality of the Church is differentiated from all other possible spiritualities, for it is a spirituality that is at the same time a sign, a testimony, a proof, that the Spirit is on this earth. Far from us to think that the Spirit only used a transient sign when He came at Pentecost; He made the hundred and twenty persons into His sign, and they would be such to the end of their mortal career: Mary the Mother of Jesus was the sign, the twelve Apostles were the sign, all the other disciples were the sign, and they were the Church. It is therefore the Church's characteristic to be and to remain forever the Pentecostal manifestation of the Spirit.

In this sense we may give countenance to an expression which is dear to not a few ecclesiastical writers; they say that the Spirit was "incarnated" in the Church, as the Second Person of the Trinity was incarnated in an individual human nature. The only exception we take to such a phrase is the use of the word "incarnate" with regard to the Spirit.

As we said in a preceding chapter, the Spirit's coming is as literal as the coming of the word: but instead of His taking flesh, He clothed Himself in signs. If those signs be permanent, the Spirit is permanently with man, as much as the Son of God is permanently with man. So the matter of supreme interest is the permanence of those features that made the first group of Christians, the assembly of the upper room, the primitive Church, into an evident sign of the Spirit. Now this is Catholicism, to hold that the Church today has the same spirituality which she had at Pentecost, otherwise she would not be the same Church; in short, she is a sign of the Spirit as authentic as the one hundred and twenty disciples.

Speaking now in an *a priori* fashion, it will be necessary for the Church if she is to be a Pentecostal sign—in other words if she is to hold the Spirit as Christ's humanity holds the divine Person—to keep forever the trance of the first Pentecost. She must be like one who is intoxicated with an entirely new life; she must speak to all men the wonderful things of God; she must be able to approach every man under the sun with the same message; she must proclaim, with an unfaltering voice, that Christ is risen from the dead and that He sits at the right hand of God, for this is the Pentecostal message, as we shall see. She must work wonders, she must have the faith of miracles, she must have ecstasies, she must, in short, understand that all prophecies have been fulfilled: the prophecy of Joel, quoted by Peter on the first outpouring of the Spirit, must be true of the Church of all times. Spiritual life must be the quality of young men and old men, great supernatural gifts must be abundant, faith in the coming judgment and the second advent of Christ must be the uninterrupted hope. Unless these things be present, no body of men, however spiritually minded, would be a true sign of the Spirit.

This is the distinction between the Old Law and the New. The just of the ancient days and the synagogue were spiritual, but they were not signs of the Spirit, even as God dwelled with the patriarchs long before He took flesh from the seed of Abraham. We say indeed in the creed that the Holy Ghost spoke through the prophets. It is strange that no symbol refers to the coming of the Holy Ghost at Pentecost as it mentions the coming down from heaven of the Son of God at His birth; the symbol professes faith in the Spirit, the Lord and the Vivifier, who proceeds from the Father and the Son, who is glorified with the Father and the Son; but where one would expect mention to be made of His having spoken through the Apostles at Pentecost, there is the declaration that He had spoken through the prophets. We might of course mean by prophets here the prophesying of the New Testament, the very phenomenon of Pentecost; but it seems more in keeping with tradition to understand by the word "prophet" here the seers of the old Law.

We must always bear in mind that the Spirit who came at Pentecost is the Spirit of promise, who had been foretold as being the great inheritance that was awaiting man. He Himself foretold His coming, for the kingdom of God, which is the burden of all ancient prophecy, is the presence of the Spirit Paraclete; Pentecost is the great fulfillment of all that had been foretold. But the Spirit in the days of the prophets did not make use of their persons as a manifest sign that He had come, He only used their tongues to foretell His advent. The Church of the New Testament, and she alone, is so constituted that whoever looks at her must say truly that the Spirit, the Lord, and Vivifier, is upon this earth. The Bride is a sign.

It is evident from the narrative of the Acts of the Apostles that the Christians, on whom the Spirit had been poured out on the fiftieth day after Christ's resurrection, kept all along in its essence that mark which the Holy Ghost had put on them; they remained spiritual in this entirely new sense of the word, with this completely fresh experience. Repeatedly the Pentecost ecstasy appears again; months and years after, men are seen in the trance which marked the first day. The Holy Ghost is everywhere; the Church prays in the Holy Ghost, acts through the Holy Ghost, arrives at decisions in union with the Holy Ghost. While Peter is yet speaking, the Holy Ghost falls on the household of Cornelius, Gentiles as they were, and they speak with tongues and magnify God. Peter, when giving an account of this conversion, expresses this perfect similarity between that event and the morning of Pentecost: "And when I had begun to speak, the Holy Ghost fell upon them, as upon us also in the beginning" (Acts 11:15).

In fact, the whole apostolic period is most evidently a continuation of Pentecost. The Apostles in their own persons, through the Spirit they had received, are a sign unto all men. But where is the end of the apostolic period? Certainly it is not at the death of the Apostles, for the Church is as apostolic today as she was when Peter was crucified on the Vatican Hill. She is as spiritual today as she was in the house of Cornelius; she fulfills in their essence all those conditions that are required of a Church that is to the Holy Ghost what the dove was to Him at Christ's baptism, an unmistakable sign of His presence.

We could here press into service in its general applications the theology of the presence of God in rational creatures. A divine Person can be said to be in a creative spirit solely on this account, because a new quality relating the creature to the divine Person has sprung up in the created spirit through divine action. If there were no such quality in man or angel, there would be no possibility of a divine presence. Consequently the Holy Ghost could not be said to abide in the Church if there were not in the Church those realities which manifested His advent at the beginning, as St. Peter puts it. If there were not in the Church sanctities of every kind and degree, congenital to the Holy Ghost, the Paraclete would not be on earth any more: Pentecost would have come to an end. Accordingly for the Church through her daily works to be a demonstration of the Spirit's activities in her is a matter of life and death. If she is not a sign of the Paraclete, she is nothing.

✠ 4 ✠

THE GREAT METAPHORS

THE CATHOLIC POSITION IS THIS, THAT THE CHURCH existed as an established society before any of those great things were written which constitute the inspired literature concerning her. The great metaphors of the Bride of the Lamb, and of the Body of Christ, and of the Building of God, which by common consent are the metaphors describing her, were the product of the inspired minds of the Apostles when the Church had already a definite history, nay, when she had even passed through her first persecution and was awaiting new hostilities from her enemies. Christ Himself spoke of the Church as the building which He would erect in the future:

> And I say to thee that thou art Peter and upon this rock I will build my church, and the gates of hell shall not prevail against it (Matt 16:18).

We may consider the parables of the kingdom as being pictures of the future Church, but Christ's utterances in His speech to Peter and in His parables are essentially concerned with a reality which did not then exist; the Son of God always alludes to a state of things that will be manifested in the future.

The apostolic utterances, on the other hand, apply to something that has already shown life and vigor, to an institution that is in the midst of the fire of persecution. It is evident that when St. Paul and St. John spoke and wrote about the Church in the way they did, everybody knew what they meant by the Church. The Church which Christ had promised had been founded; and the Christians of the early period were conscious of this, that they were the Church, that the inspired images which have become classical style in the matter were put forward concerning a Church which they themselves constituted. They knew themselves to be that Body of which Christ was the Head, they knew themselves to be that Bride who, with the Spirit said, "Come."

It is evident to begin with the very last image of Christian prophecy—that when St. John said, at the end of his Revelation, "And the Spirit and the Bride said: Come" (Rev 22:17), he was speaking of the Christian Church that surrounded him, he was alluding to a life that was going on before his eyes. He was not primarily concerned with the distant future, for the concluding sentences of his Apocalypse are exhortations which were meant for those who would hear and read the prophesy at the time it was uttered:

> And he that heareth, let him say: Come. And he that thirsteth, let him come. And he that will, let him take the water of life, freely. For I testify to everyone that heareth the words of the prophecy of this book. If any man shall add to these things, God shall add unto him the plagues written in this book. And if any man shall take away from the words of the book of this proph-

ecy, God shall take away his part out of the book of life, and out
of the holy city, and from these things that are written in this
book. He that giveth testimony of these things, saith: Surely, I
come quickly: Amen. Come Lord Jesus. The grace of our Lord
Jesus Christ be with you all. Amen (Rev 22:17-21).

Likewise St. Paul has in view the immediate spiritual interest of
his Christians; he is anxious to enlighten all men,

that they may see what is the dispensation of the mystery which
has been hidden from eternity in God, who created all things.
That the manifold wisdom of God may be made known to the
principalities and powers in heavenly places through the church
(Eph 3:9-10).

It is all actuality. St. Paul enumerates the elements of the Christian
election; he tells his converts to what heights of grace they have been
raised. Have we not to take it for granted, however, that, lofty as his
considerations are, they are not beyond his hearers? He was speaking
language that was familiar to Christians, that was, in fact, their staple
of spiritual life. When, therefore, he spoke of Christ as being Head
over all the Church and when he called the Church, Christ's Body, he
was readily understood; the metaphor entered into the daily life of his
hearers, the high simile had become the norm of practical conduct,
for all spiritual work consisted in "the perfecting of the saints, the
work of the ministry, the edifying of the Body of Christ" (Eph 4:12).

From the metaphor of the Body, St. Paul, in the same breath almost, can pass on to the metaphor of the Bride, which is more properly the image of St. John. Again, with a directly practical purpose,
Paul speaks of Christ as loving His Church as husbands love their

wives in all things. St. Paul never uses the word Bride: this title is exclusively bestowed by St. John, but in his Epistle to the Ephesians he gives a description of the Church which is entirely couched in nuptial terms.

St. Paul has a third metaphor which occurs only once: the Church is the House of God, the Pillar and ground of the truth. It is obvious in this case also that Timothy, to whom these words were addressed, was familiar with the idea of the Church as a building erected by God, in which the Christian had his spiritual being:

> That thou mayest know how thou oughtest to behave thyself in the house of God, which is the church of the living God, the pillar and ground of the truth (1 Tim 3:15).

Did St. Paul complete Christ's own words: "I shall build up my Church"?

The metaphors then presuppose, in apostolic literature, a well-known reality, something so clearly defined that it could be expressed figuratively without detriment to its constitutional perfection. So we have from the very beginning this double aspect of the Church: she is, firstly, an actual society, well definable. Secondly, things are predicated concerning her which are so high that no language will suffice except figurative language. The society is first, its metaphorical description is second. The Christians of the days of Paul and John are that very Church about whom such incredible things are said.

There is not a Church of actuality and a Church of metaphor, much less are there only metaphors without any corresponding reality; no, something has appeared here on earth, indescribably beautiful, as wonderful as anything God ever created, something that manifests the glory of God, as the mysterious personality of Christ manifests the glory of God: "to Him be glory in the Church and in Christ Jesus" (Eph 3:21). The titles "House of God, pillar and ground of truth," "Body of Christ," "Bride of Christ" are appropriate terms.

When St. John, then, looking forward now to the consummation of all things, is given to see the Bride of the Lamb, all the glories of heaven and earth, of the human world and of the angelic world are united in that figure:

> And there came one of the seven angels, who had the vials full
> of the seven last plagues, and spoke with me, saying: Come and I
> will show thee the Bride, the wife of the Lamb (Rev 21:9).

The Christians knew that in this great imagery was predicted their final triumph through the power of God; they were and would be that heavenly Jerusalem, that Bride of the Lamb, that City of God.

Was it easy for the Christians of those days to find themselves thus depicted? Was it not asking too much of them thus to think of themselves in images so glorious and so unearthly? It does not appear that there was any strangeness to their minds in the apostolic and apocalyptic language. That whole age was under the impression of the exceeding greatness of the Christian vocation. When St. Paul prays that the Ephesians may be able to comprehend what is the breadth and the length and the height and the depth of the mystery of Christ's charity, he asks for a privilege that is common to all the saints, that is to say, to all the faithful: "You may be able to comprehend with all the saints" (Eph 3:18).

The metaphors of which we speak here are taken from the risen life of Christ, from His glorious life. As the risen God, Christ is Head:

And he is the head of the body, the Church who is the beginning, the firstborn from the dead, that in all things he may hold
the primacy (Col 1:18).

Likewise the Bride is the Bride of the risen Christ:

And I, John, saw the holy city, the new Jerusalem, coming down
out of heaven from God prepared as a bride adorned for her
husband (Rev 21:2).

So too, the image of the House of God, of the Pillar and the
ground of the truth, in the mind of St. Paul is associated with the
mystery of glorification, for he completes the metaphor with these
words:

And evidently great is the mystery of godliness, which was manifested in the flesh, was justified in the spirit, appeared unto angels, hath been preached to the Gentiles, is believed in the world,
is taken up in glory (1 Tim 3:16).

It would be easy to work out more completely the full meaning of
those metaphors; the Fathers and other preachers have left wonderful
enlargements of the original ideas. But like all metaphors, their power
is in their very simplicity. When we are told that the Church is the
Body of the glorified Christ, that she is the Bride of Christ, we hardly
need more. We know that nothing greater could be said, that the supreme point of intimacy has been reached. We realize that whatever
theology may say in more precise language will not be deeper or ho-
lier than the contents of the metaphor.

But the Church thus pictured with the brush of divine inspiration
had, as we said, all along her real, organized, clearly-governed life. It

was known from practical test who were those who could in any way be said to belong to the Body of Christ; it was recognized which assembly of human beings deserved the supreme honor of being called the Bride of Christ; it was clear to all which was that House of God in which Christians worked out their salvation. So the Church has her own definition of herself; she can formulate her nature in a clear phrase; she is not a vague reality, she knows who are hers and who are not hers, for this clearness of distinction between the believer and the unbeliever is one of the most marked qualities of the early Church and of the Church of all times. She knows who are those who are within and those who are without. Her whole ethical life is based on this realization of membership, of brotherhood:

> Know you not that your bodies are the members of Christ? Shall I then take the members of Christ and make them the members of an harlot? God forbid! Or know you not that he who is joined to a harlot is made one body? For they shall be, saith he, two in one flesh. But he who is joined to the Lord is one spirit (1 Cor 6:15-17).

The Apostles, in their disciplinary rulings, realized clearly that their power was only over such as were within:

> For what have I to do to judge them that are without? Do not you judge them that are within? For them that are without, God will judge. Put away the evil one from among yourselves (1 Cor 5:12-13).

With inspired elaborateness St. Paul, in his second Epistle to Corinth, works out further the idea of the division between the Church and everything else:

Bear not the yoke with unbelievers. For what participation hath justice with injustice? Or what fellowship hath light with darkness? And what concord hath Christ with Belial? Or what part hath the faithful with the unbeliever? And what agreement hath the temple of God with idols? For you are the temple of the living God; as God saith: I will dwell in them and walk among them. And I will be their God: and they shall be my people. Wherefore: Go out from among them and be ye separate, saith the Lord, and touch not the unclean thing. And I will receive you. And I will be a Father to you: and you shall be my sons and daughters, saith the Lord Almighty (2 Cor 6:14-18).

How then has the Church defined herself? We might say, through a self-assertion of centuries. The Catholic Church knows herself with a precision that is truly astonishing and she knows her boundaries with a clearness one might almost call geographical. The Church can define herself as the assembly of the faithful, living in the oneness of faith, under one Head, Christ, in one government whose center is the Roman See. This is what we might call the "farthest limit," the *Ultima Thule* of the Church. Whoever does not conform to those elementary requirements is not of the Church. But the Church when she gives thus her theological precisions, does not limit herself on the ascending plane; she will quite readily define herself also as the society of all the elect who are already confirmed in eternal charity, be they angels, be they the spirits of men. But the metaphors of which we speak here cover the whole definition of the Church; in fact they are vaster than any possible definition.

It has been suggested sometimes that the idealization of the Church which is contained in the metaphors is justified then only if the great images are supposed to represent the Church in her glory, the elect in heaven. In such a case it is evident that no picture is too brilliant, as the condition of the elect in heaven is holy and perfect beyond description. But it is obvious that these symbols must be applied to the Church of the present time; we do not exclude the glorified Church from the circle of the image; one and the same picture gives us the Church in her various states, the state of struggle and the state of glory. This is why the Church is so beautiful; she is truly the strong Body of Christ, she is truly the Bride of the Conqueror of souls, she is the fullness of Him who ascended above all the heavens, who has filled all things with the strength of His sanctity; she is a pillar of truth that reaches from earth to heaven.

In this connection much could be said concerning the applicability to the Church, even in her present state, of some of the tableaux of St. John's vision in the Apocalypse. I have refrained from making use of those descriptions and calling them metaphors; they are more truly pictures of the people of God themselves, in their state of struggle, of sanctity, of triumph. We have the great vision of the innumerable multitude "which no man could number, of all nations and tribes and peoples and tongues, standing before the throne and in sight of the Lamb, clothed with white robes, and palms in their hands" (Rev 7:9). Then we are told of "them that had overcome the beast and his image and the number of his name, standing on the sea of glass, having the harps of God: and singing the canticle of Moses, the servant of God, and the canticle of the Lamb" (Rev 15:2-3). Once more, we have the description of the "Lamb standing upon mount Zion, and with him an hundred forty-four thousand, having his name and the name of his Father written on their foreheads" (Rev 14:1).

Magnificent as the tableaux are, they may be taken to mean the present Church as much as the Church in heaven, the one, undivided Church whose sanctity is eternal life, that eternal life which is already possessed by us here on earth. There are features in those tableaux which are applicable only to the final state of security in heaven, but there are as many traits which can only be found in the Church on earth. All those holy ones right through the visions of St. John are engaged in washing their robes in the Blood of the Lamb, a purification that makes them worthy of Christ but which is evidently the operation of this life:

> Behold, I come quickly: and my reward is with me, to render to every man according to his works. I am Alpha and Omega, the First and the Last, the Beginning and the End. Blessed are they that wash their robes in the blood of the Lamb: that they may have a right to the tree of life and may enter in by the gates into the city (Rev 22:12).

✠ 5 ✠

The Christ of the Bride

The Church is the Bride, not of the Holy Ghost but of the Second Person of the Trinity, the Son of God Incarnate. She is essentially the Bride of the Lamb, of the One who from the heights of heaven fights the great battle against Satan and the Beast. It is the mission of the Holy Ghost to make the Church a fit bride; to give her the heart of a bride, the mind of a bride, the body of a bride. Without the Holy Ghost no association of saintly people could be called the bride of the Lamb. In this book on the Spirit and the Bride we presuppose all that Christ has done as the Savior of His Body, that is to say, the Church. We also presuppose all that Christ is today and will be for eternity to the Church. We are intent on bringing into light that mysterious partnership of the Spirit and the Bride which enables her to be worthy of the Bridegroom, Christ.

The first question that presents itself is this: how does the Church apprehend her Bridegroom, how does she think of Him, how does she picture Him to herself through the inspiration of the Holy Spirit?

It is evident from even a superficial study of the Church's history that the Christian people have not a monotonous, lifeless, unvaried way of expressing their Christ. Without any doubt, one may be permitted to distinguish between the objective and the subjective presentment of Christ. The Church has both and always has had both.

The objective Christ is the Son of God, made Man, in His real, natural existence. There were the thirty-three years of His mortal life, there were the three days of His death, there were the forty days of His risen life on this earth, there is now and forever His glorious and impassible life, in power and majesty, at the right hand of God. These years and these endless aeons of life are the objective reality. Of this objective existence of Christ few human beings can be said to have been witness. The thirty years from the nativity at Bethlehem to the baptism by John were passed in great obscurity. The period from the baptism to the ascension was Christ's public life. Of this Peter the Apostle speaks with due appreciation as representing the official mission of the Master; the condition of apostleship is this, to have been with Christ during those years:

> Wherefore of these men who have companied with us, all the time that the Lord Jesus came in and went out among us, Beginning from the baptism of John, until the day wherein he was taken up from us, one of these must be made a witness with us of his resurrection (Acts 1:21-22).

No human being has beheld Christ in His glory with the eyes of the flesh unless he were transported by the Spirit. Stephen the deacon indeed, when looking steadfastly to heaven, saw the glory of God and Jesus standing on the right hand of God. This great vision was vouchsafed to the first martyr when he was still in the flesh; but the writer of the Acts is careful to note that such a transport was possible only because Stephen was "full of the Holy Ghost" (Acts 7:55).

Christ in the sacrament of the Eucharist is also the objective Christ, as His existence in the sacramental state is independent of man's faith in Him.

How have the various generations of the faithful of Christ apprehended their Lord and Master in these His natural and historic existences? Have they succeeded in portraying Him to themselves adequately? Is there a traditional view of the Incarnate Son of God in His earthly life? Moreover, is there any possibility of catching a truthful glimpse of the heavenly life?

We must admit, of course, as an *a priori* assumption that the Spirit would never allow the Bride to go astray in this portraying to herself of the One she loves; is it not the primary office of the Spirit to manifest the Son after His departure from this planet? "Yet a little while and the world seeth me no more. But you see me: because I live, and you shall live" (John 14:19). This vision of the absent Jesus is rendered possible through the Spirit. So we have to maintain that the Catholic way of representing, of imagining the Son of God in the various phases of His objective existence is, in the main, true. The Church not only reads the deeds of Christ and remembers His words, but she has actually a mental vision of Him whilst on earth, a characterization which is as true as it is beautiful. She would recognize instinctively a false character sketch of Him, if such were attempted. We all know how, given the same written documents concerning Christ's career, it is possible to conjure up most diverse mental pictures of Him, to indulge in most varied views of His character.

Now I say that the Church had a true perception through all the centuries: she knew Him to be One who is meek and humble of heart. But this can never be more than an outline. No man, without some special mystical gifts, can enter into the profundities of Christ's human life among men.

There is, I think, great stability and truthfulness in this sentimental and imaginative representation of the Incarnate God. It is often said that with the advent of the Catholic humanism of the Franciscan period there was developed a new way of visualizing Christ: it is most commonly called "the devotion to Christ's humanity." If pressed too far, this division into periods might leave the impression that the sentimental, the imaginative, nay, even the intellectual apprehension of Christ by earlier generations was deficient in warmth, rendered a harder picture of the Savior. Such a superficial mapping out of the past life of the Church would be truly intolerable if it were taken literally. It would mean at bottom that the successive generations of Christians are not vivified by the same Spirit, that at one time the faithful apprehended the Lord and Master less truly than at other times. Moreover, historically, this easy division has no *locus standi*, "place to stand." Let anyone read the Homilies of St. John Chrysostom, for instance, and he will see for himself what Christ was to the men that listened to the great Greek preacher, the men of the fourth century. The difference in this matter between the fourth century and the thirteenth is more apparent than real.

We do not here touch upon the question whether the Church has it in her power to evoke the physical image of her Christ, whether she can paint a true portrait of His exterior, His lineaments, His whole external behavior. We all seem to know how we should have liked Him to have looked, and without hesitation we should reject certain attempts at His portraiture as blasphemous abominations.

Coming now to the Church's contact with and representation of the Son of God in the glories of heaven, it is evident that the vision of so great a majesty is beyond all human capacity; no man, no saint, could behold Christ in the splendor of the Father and live. It will require the glorified state in the elect to enable them to behold the unveiled face of their Lord. Nevertheless the Church has her own gift from the Spirit so as to make her capable of thinking and speaking worthily of the Son of man in His might. In St. John's Apocalypse, the Spirit shows Himself a supreme artist whenever He introduces the word of God, the glorified Redeemed. Christian art through the centuries has not proved unworthy of the divine Master, the Spirit, who showed to John the Lamb and the Lamb's Bride. With very rare and late exceptions the Church's art has observed a virginal *pudeur*, "modesty," and has been preserved from the arrogance of an unprayerful naturalism. The pictorial representation of the Son of God in majesty has been chiefly emblematic and of the prophetic style, the Son of man being shown just throwing out hints of the power that is in Him, without any hopeless effort on the part of the artist to make Him appear in the splendor that is His native glory. Are not the severe presentments of the Son of God in majesty in the apses of the ancient basilicas an indication of a more delicate appreciation of Christ's position on the part of the Christians who created that art than the modern attempt to make the All-Holy look as humanly benign as possible? Very great love despairs of expressing adequately the beloved, and symbols are welcome, to act as a shelter for a tenderness greater than words can say or the artist's hand can depict.

Entering now into that portion of the Church's life which I have called the subjective Christ, I feel that I am treading on very sacred but also very burning ground; it is the presence of the Son of God in the thorn-bush of human psychology. For unless we reject all Catholic hagiography and much of Catholic devotional life we have to admit the reality of a Christ-presence in the Christian people that is neither the natural and personal existence of the word Incarnate nor the infinitely mysterious sacramental presence. Innumerable believers and saints of all grades have had Christ made present to them not in the measure of His glory, but in the measure of their own souls, in proportion to their capacity of holding Him; under forms that are more truly an expression of their own personalities than of the Personality of Christ. To quote well-known instances from Catholic hagiography, it seems evident that the Christ who dwelt in the heart of St. Gertrude is different from the Christ that filled the imagination of St. Theresa, and both those lovers of the Son of God differ greatly in their descriptions of their Beloved from St. Margaret Mary, the apostle of the humiliated heart of Christ. Quite a different Christ seems to speak in the virgin of Avila from the Christ who speaks in the virgin of *Paray-le-Monial.* I call this Christ the subjective Christ because He is really to the holy soul a present personality, not only the thought or the image of Him who is in the glory above. When St. Margaret Mary breaks forth into matchless condolence for the neglected Christ, she is not doing anything retrospective, as a remembrance of the mortal life of Jesus; she is too great a realist for that. She has, on the contrary, found her Spouse neglected by the Christians of her own days; she meets Him bleeding and sorrowful, and she takes Him away in the arms of her love to console Him.

With this overwhelming cloud of mystical happenings right through the ages of the Church, it becomes imperative to assign a cause and to enunciate a principle. Shall we say then that it is the Spirit who makes Christ live in the hearts of chosen men and women according to their capacity, and that moreover the Spirit impresses the sentiment and the effective powers of Christians differently at different times; that He truly creates in them a Christ entirely in conformity with that truth which is His very essence, yet with wonderful variety?

The total Christ is in Heaven, not only in the totality of His double nature but also in the totality of His character. No one here on earth can make such a totality his own. So the Spirit breaks up that glory, as the prism breaks up the white light, and infinite varieties of the Christ Person are received by the saints as their own share in the boundless mystery of the Son of God. Not that the Christian soul ever forgets what faith tells us as to the immensity of Christ's greatness. But the taste of Him by the soul, the vision of Him by the eyes of the spirit, the holding of Him through loving affection, must be partial, as our faculties in this life do not possess that unlimited expansion of strength which will be theirs in the state of glory in heaven. The Jesus who converses familiarly with a saint is a creation of the Holy Ghost in the mind of the one thus favored, an impression produced by the Spirit of truth, yet a true reality, not a fantastic illusion, as such a grace is a genuine communication with Christ Himself, as if His voice were heard from a distance.

The presence of Jesus in the Church through the Spirit is one of the beauties of the Christian dispensation. The mystery of that presence is rendered comprehensible, as mysteries may be comprehensible, through the union between the Incarnate Son of God and the Holy Ghost. This our Lord promised when He said of the Paraclete:

> He shall glorify me: because he shall receive of mine and shall show it to you. All things whatsoever the Father hath are mine.

> Therefore I said that he shall receive of mine and show it to you
> (John 16:14-15).

A presence of that kind is naturally not thinkable outside the Christian dogma of the Incarnation and the indwelling of God in man through grace.

Once, then, we accept this possibility of Christ's subjective presence in the souls purified by His grace, we may be ready for any spiritual marvel, and above all, for any variety of spiritual marvels. The Bride will abound in the sense of Christ, she will see in Him the most varied perfections, she will say of Him:

> My beloved is white and ruddy, chosen out of thousands. His head is as the finest gold: His locks as branches of palm trees, black as a raven (Cant 10:10-11).

It is within the power of the Bride to conjure up the past of her Spouse, His desolation in His death, and to console Him as if it were an actual event; she can even place Him, in her sweet imagination of love, in hypothetical situations, and tell Him what she would do for Him if He were thus beset by enemies. Lovers have those powers. With Peter's fervor, but with more humility than Peter then showed, the faithful soul can say, even today, "Lord, I am ready to go with thee, both into prison and to death" (Luke 22:33). The Lord of glory is eternally free from all bonds and from death, yet many Christian souls find it sweet to speak to Him words similar to those of St. Peter, because, if the Lord *per impossibile*, "impossibly," were to fall again into the hands of His enemies, their conduct would show that loving fidelity. We can make such hypothetical acts of heroicity with the Beloved of our souls. For when we have thus fed on His countenance as the Spirit has imprinted it on our consciousness, we remember all at once that He is worlds apart from human conditions, that no image of Him in our soul can do Him justice. We want Him to fly away from all human limitations, and we say to Him with the bride of the Canticle: *fuge, dilecte mi,* "Flee away, O my beloved" (Cant 8:14). we worship Him as the God who has ascended above all the heavens and from thence will come to judge the living and the dead. With St. Paul we realize keenly that although Jesus was "crucified through weakness, yet he liveth by the power of God" (2 Cor 13:4). Not one of the great and terrible things which the seer of Patmos says of the anger of the Lamb and the awfulness of His majesty would the Church want to be unsaid. To the Bride's ears the prophecies of the coming of Christ in power are like sweet music:

> And the heaven departed as a book folded up. And every mountain, and the islands, were moved out of their places. And the kings of the earth and the princes and tribunes and the rich and the strong and every bondman and every freeman hid themselves in the dens and in the rocks of mountains: And they say to the mountains and the rocks: Fall upon us and hide us from the face of him that sitteth upon the throne and from the wrath of the Lamb. For the great day of their wrath is come. And who shall be able to stand (Rev 6:14-17)?

✠ 6 ✠

THE RESURRECTION CHURCH

IT IS EVIDENT THAT THE HOLY GHOST WAS GIVEN ON THE first Pentecost in intimate connection with the career of Christ the Son of God. Christ's words concerning the coming of the Spirit leave no doubt on that subject; likewise the declarations of the Apostles, chiefly of St. Peter, are most emphatic: the Spirit has come in connection with the Christ whom the Jewish people had denied. It is very necessary for us to remember this aspect of the descent of the Holy Ghost; from the moment of His coming to the end of times, nay, for all eternity, He will be to the Church the Spirit of Jesus. It is His work and His mission to manifest the Jesus who has been taken away, who has hidden His glory and who Himself refrained from declaring to the world the greatness that was in Him: the Spirit has to do it all until the Lord come in the full splendor of His glory. In one word, the glorification of Jesus has not been seen by the world; it is the Spirit that glorifies Christ or more accurately still, He is the glorification.

John the Apostle, when writing his Gospel many years after the day of Pentecost, and looking back on his own wonderful career in the kingdom of Christ, saw quite clearly this intimate connection between the Holy Ghost and the resurrection of the Master. He remembered the dark days when the mission of Jesus aroused so much hostility. There was not then the experimental knowledge of divine mysteries which had been granted since, so lavishly: "For as yet the Spirit was not given, because Jesus was not yet glorified" (John 7:39). The Lord standing in the midst of the crowds on the great festival, with a loud voice had promised the coming of the Spirit under the symbol of living waters:

> And on the last and great day of the festivity, Jesus stood and cried, saying: If any man thirst, let him come to me and drink. He that believeth in me, as the scripture saith: Out of his belly shall flow rivers of living water. Now this he said of the Spirit which they should receive who believed in him (John 7:37-39).

But what had prevented the Master who could do all things from bestowing then, in His own lifetime, that supremely desirable gift? The answer is: the Spirit is essentially and unalterably the radiation in this world of Christ's glorification: "For as yet the Spirit was not given, because Jesus was not yet glorified." So we hear Peter proclaim aloud that all that happened at Pentecost happened because Jesus was in the glory of the Father through the resurrection and the ascension; St. Peter's speech on that occasion of occasions is all about Christ's resurrection from the dead:

> This Jesus has God raised again, whereof all we are witnesses. Being exalted therefore by the right hand of God and having

received of the Father the promise of the Holy Ghost, he (Jesus) has poured forth this which you see and hear (Acts 2:32-33).

Let us consider for one moment the expression, "And having received of the Father the promise of the Holy Ghost." It is evidently the Son who has received from the Father the promise of the Holy Ghost; this can only mean that the Son was then empowered to pour forth on the earth that glorious thing which was the promise of all times—the Spirit. And in this He showed His exaltation, that exaltation which He had refused to show in His own Person to the eyes of the world. The Spirit, then, is truly the Spirit of Christ's exaltation.

The doctrine of the resurrection and Christ's glorification in heaven is the message that runs right through the Acts of the Apostles. Stephen full of the Holy Ghost, looks up steadfastly to heaven where he sees the glory of God and Jesus standing on the right hand of God. Whenever the Spirit falls like a torrent on the Christian community, they break forth into a canticle of Christ's power:

> And now, Lord, behold their threatenings: and grant unto thy servants that with all confidence they may speak thy word. By stretching forth thy hand to cures and signs and wonders, to be done by the name of thy holy Son, Jesus. And when they had prayed, the place was moved wherein they were assembled: and they were all filled with the Holy Ghost: and they spoke the word of God with confidence (Acts 4:29-31).

The Son of God in the power of the Spirit had come near them in glory and majesty; His resurrection from the dead was to the Christians an event of intensely greater interest now that they had received the Spirit than when it actually took place. Above all, the coming of the Spirit was a miracle of such magnificence and such perseverance that no man could deny it. And that miracle was an irrepressible proclamation of the triumph of Jesus, whom the Jews had denied before Pilate and whom they had crucified.

Christ was already in the state of glory though not yet at the right hand of the Father when for the last time on this earth, He made His declaration concerning the mission of the Spirit:

> And eating together with them, he commanded them that they should not depart from Jerusalem, but should wait for the promise of the Father, which you have heard (saith he) by my mouth. For John indeed baptized with water: but you shall be baptized with the Holy Ghost, not many days hence (Acts 1:4-5).

He himself reminds them of what He had said in the days of His mortality only forty days before. The promise of the Father, the coming of the Holy Ghost, is the crowning event of Christ's own career on this earth. The disciples were not prepared for the kingdom of the Spirit: they were ready now, after witnessing the miracle of the resurrection, to accept as a near event the kingdom in which Christ would be visibly a king:

> They therefore who were come together asked him, saying: Lord, wilt thou at this time restore again the kingdom to Israel (Acts 1:6)?

Most energetically the Lord rejects such an idea: it is not at all the plan of God. Another empire, not less solid, not less vast, will be established not many days hence: the empire of the Spirit:

> But he said to them: It is not for you to know the times or mo-

ments, which the Father hath put in his own power: but you shall receive the power of the Holy Ghost coming upon you, and you shall be witnesses unto me in Jerusalem, and in all Judea and Samaria, and even to the uttermost part of the earth (Acts 1:7-8).

He, the risen Lord, does not show forth in His own Person His resurrection as He might have done so easily; but does this mean that the resurrection mystery is to remain hidden from the world? Nothing of the kind. They will be the witnesses of Christ's new life, but witnesses not in their own strength but in the power of the Holy Ghost. The Lord had said before His passion:

But when the Paraclete cometh, whom I will send you from the Father, the Spirit of truth, who proceedeth from the Father, he shall give testimony of me. And you shall give testimony, because you are with me from the beginning (John 15:26-27).

It is not without deep significance that this final pronouncement of the Son of God concerning the Spirit was made by Him, as we said, when He had already in Himself the complete glory of His resurrection. So great is the mission of the Spirit that even the risen Son of God leaves it to Him to manifest His name.

In order to bring out fully this office of the Spirit to be an unassailable testimony of Christ's resurrection and ascension, one ought to comment extensively upon the Lord's discourses after the Last Supper, when He declares that His departure is expedient: "For if I go not, the Paraclete will not come to you: but if I go, I will send him to you" (John 16:7). The office of the Spirit in this world is stated in the words we read so often but whose meaning no man can completely fathom:

When he is come, he will convince the world of sin and of justice and of judgment. Of sin: because they believed not in me. And of justice: because I go to the Father: and you shall see me no longer. And of judgment: because the prince of this world is already judged (John 16:8-11).

The Spirit is described by our Lord as one who will take the whole world to task; He will be a power that cannot be ignored, He will be a triumph which men have to accept in spite of themselves; above all, He will be to the disciples themselves a strengthening of the intellect that will enable them to accept courageously the whole mystery of man's salvation in all its aspects. He will convince the world of sin: there will be the very clear division between the believer and the unbeliever; there will be this marvel, which the world itself will have to accept, that One who has gone away to the Father, that One who is seen no longer, is after all the greatest power in this world. There will be such security of hope amongst the believers that it will be apparent to all eyes that the Prince of darkness, the Prince of this world, is already judged. The Christian will not walk in terror of that evil power, he will be as one who is completely at his ease in all his movements; the feeling of triumph will be an integral feature of his sanctity. It will be a characteristic of the faithful to take without questioning the validity of very great truths: beliefs that would frighten man were he left to himself will come to them quite naturally, theirs will be a vastness of outlook which will embrace heaven and earth, all the marvels of God's goodness and all the terrors of God's justice. The Christian people will have great intuitions, marvellous anticipations of the future, they will truly be a race of heroes and seers. Above all the Spirit will reveal to the world the whole substance of Christ, all those marvels which the Son of God while He was here on earth kept in reserve without showing them. He will be to the Church the great teacher of the mystery of Christ; there will be no doubts any more as to the personality of Christ, as to His two-fold nature, as to His office of Redeemer, as to His power as Lord and Judge. All those supreme truths the Church will hold as by instinct; for it is the very nature of the Spirit Himself to receive all things from the Son, as the Son has received all things from the Father.

The passage we are commenting upon may indeed be called the constitution of the kingdom of the Spirit; nowhere else is the power and the solidity of this new world described with stronger force of language. There is no efficacy of ruling which is denied to the Spirit; He rules over the pagan world, He rules over the Christian world, He reveals to man the glories of heaven and the terrors of hell; He is the proclamation of the victory of Christ and of the discomfiture of the Spirit of darkness. In one word, He is truly the kingdom of God amongst men.

Our conclusion, then, must be that the Spirit of Pentecost is the Spirit of the resurrection and that His testimony is the testimony of the glorification of Christ. But from this follows another truth of paramount importance: that the Church is intrinsically, by every law of her constitution, the Church of the resurrection. She is the sign of Christ's resurrection because she has in herself all the qualities of that resurrection. Unless the Church were an integral portion of the mystery of the resurrection she would not be the Church which was founded at Pentecost, because Pentecost was the crowning of the resurrection.

We might view the Church differently, we might think of her as an assembly of faithful believers who are imitating Christ in His lowliness; we might think of her as being in the same condition in which the disciples were when they followed the Lord in the days of His public mission. If we thought of her in such terms exclusively we should be really wrong, because it would take away from the Church the element of actuality; she would not be in immediate contact with the Christ as He is now, through the resurrection; she would be chiefly commemorative, or perhaps also anticipatory, in the sense that she would remember the Christ as He was in the past, or that she would hope see Him one day as He will be in the glory of the future.

If the risen Christ had remained here on earth as He was during the forty days, and had become the visible center of the Church, then evidently the Church would have been outwardly the Church of the resurrection. All her actuality, all her life would have been in conformity with her risen God. She would have remembered unceasingly the nativity, the temporal life, the passion and the death of the risen Emmanuel; but her contact would have been with the Son of God, not in the form of a slave but in the form of glorified Godhead. Now, as we said, Christ withdrew His glorified Person from this earth with a great gesture of finality. Has it then become impossible for the Church to be a resurrection Church otherwise than by faith? Through the mystery of the Spirit we say that the Church has not been the loser through Christ's departure. She is as much in contact with the resurrection mystery as if the risen Savior were among us still, because the Spirit is essentially a glorifier, that is to say, one who makes Christ's glory a reality here on earth. He is not a glorifier in words merely, but a glorifier because through Him the very substance of glory takes up its abode with men.

Very different will be our view of the Church as we understand this extension of the resurrection mystery through the Spirit into the

Church. We are not disciples who follow the Lord on the dusty road during His public ministry, we are not even disciples who eat and drink with Him during the forty days that follow Easter, but we are the elect of God, who walk with the risen Christ in newness of life, that newness of life which the Apostles themselves did not possess till the Spirit came down upon them at Pentecost. In many ways, of course, we imitate the disciples as they are the companions of the mortal Christ and the risen Christ before the ascension, but such an imitation, however high a spirituality it may be, is far from being a total Christianity. We actually share in Christ's risen life, we share in Christ's ascension; we are not only His friends and admirers in those auspicious periods of His wonderful career:

> But God (who is rich in mercy) for his exceeding charity where-
> with he loved us even when we were dead in sins, hath quickened
> us together in Christ (by whose grace you are saved). And hath
> raised us up together and hath made us sit together in the heav-
> enly places, through Christ Jesus (Eph 2:4-6).

The Spirit of glorification was Christ's reward. St. Peter assures us that Christ received the Spirit of promise. That Spirit of promise is poured out on us also. Unless we consider the Church as being rooted and established in the resurrection from the dead of the Son of God, through the Spirit of glory, our notions of the Church will not exceed the human measure. She will be only an assembly of holy people when she ought to be a function of Christ's risen life.

✠ 7 ✠

THE EVERLASTING SPIRIT AND THE BIRTH OF THE BRIDE

IT IS OFTEN ASKED, "WHAT IS THE PECULIAR SIGNIFICANCE of the coming of the Spirit at Pentecost, as there seem to be so many other ways in which He comes to the sons of men. Did not the Spirit manifest Himself frequently, even before Pentecost? Was He not the Spirit of the prophets of old? Was He not the Spirit that came over the Son of God at His baptism? Did not Christ say on the resurrection day: "Receive ye the Holy Ghost" (John 20:22), when He breathed on the disciples?

It is one of the original features of the whole Christian dispensation that it deals in realities which are everlasting on the one hand and which, on the other hand, have all the glory of a new revelation for which the world has been waiting. For not a few, this apparent newness in the fundamental permanence is a real difficulty. Thus, for instance, the Christian is asked to consider the hour in which Christ died as one of the turning points in the history of the world, because mankind was redeemed in that supreme moment. But he is also told to believe that for centuries before, in fact right from the beginning of mankind, salvation has been operative. Adam and Eve were saved in Christ. So again, the coming of the Gospel is celebrated as an event that is entirely new; Christ Himself told His disciples to consider themselves blessed to see what they saw, to hear what they heard, because many kings and many saints had wished to see and hear those very things and the privilege had not been granted to them. On the other hand the patriarchs and the prophets, the whole Church of the Primitives, as St. Paul calls them, had a revelation which made them happy.

The explanation is that it has not been God's plan to make darkest night be succeeded by light, but to make the fainter light lead up to the great light, because at no time—again in the words of St. Paul in the Acts—did God leave Himself without witnesses. But the fullness of light when it does come is a mercy so great that all that has preceded it is as night by comparison. Such is evidently the characteristic of that divine relativity. The dispensation of God is in reality a family affair; God only deals with His own family, and the events of great solemnity are as family joys; some life there has been and some happiness there has been from the very beginning. But as in the family the birth of a child seems to make the parents forget all their former happiness, so in the Christian dispensation, the birth of the Son of God, with all it implies, makes the past history of the family of God stand out like a long and tedious expectation.

We may apply to the whole history of the divine dispensation that law which Christ enunciates more than once, the law of the kingdom of heaven:

> For he that hath, to him shall be given, and he shall abound: but he that hath not, from him shall be taken away that also which he hath (Matt 13:12).

God only deals in life, not in death; and the events of God's dealing with man are degrees of life, as the higher life succeeds the weaker life or as consummate life follows upon the preparation for it.

In nothing is this great rule of the kingdom of heaven more constantly realized than in the mystery of the Spirit. If there is one evident impression left on the student of the Scriptures it is this: the coming of the Spirit at the first Pentecost was meant to be an entirely new event and also a final one. No other incident of equal magnitude has ever existed in the realm of the Spirit, nor will there be another supernatural event as great, till Christ comes in glory and majesty, to judge the living and the dead. But from these same Scriptures we know that the Spirit was no stranger here on earth, that He had been at work at all times. On the resurrection day Christ had breathed on the apostles and had told them expressly: "Receive ye the Holy Ghost" (John 20:22). The same divine Person had been seen hovering over Christ Himself after He had been baptized by John. Christ's enemies were sinning against the Holy Ghost when they would not receive the words of the Son of God; the Holy Ghost had come on Mary when she conceived in the womb; the Holy Ghost had spoken through the prophets; the Holy Ghost had been brooding over the waters from the very beginning.

And there is more: it is part of the Catholic faith to believe that men were justified and saved right through the ages; the elect before the coming of Christ formed an innumerable people coming from the Gentiles and the Jewish family. Their sanctity was like our sanctity: faith, hope, and charity, three powers that spring from the very root of sanctification, i.e. sanctifying grace. In all of those saints, just as in ourselves when we are in the blessed state of grace, there was dwelling the blessed Trinity, Father, Son, and Holy Ghost. Within their created spirit there was that marvel of marvels which is called in theology the "invisible mission of the divine Persons." The Second Person and the Third Person were being granted to them from the Father as their possession; for such is Christian sanctity everlastingly, at all times, before the Incarnation, before the first Pentecost, as well as in the days following those divine events. The presence of the Trinity in the justified soul is a doctrine we have to believe, and that presence of the Second Person and the Third Person is called their "invisible mission," in opposition to their visible advents which took place when the word was incarnated and when the Holy Ghost appeared at Pentecost.

We have therefore an accumulation of divine realities in the Christian dispensation which may appear to some bewildering. It is truly a disconcerting application of the amazing principle which God alone, who is rich unto all, could follow as His policy: "He that hath, to him shall be given and he shall abound" (Matt 25:29). Still it is nonetheless certain that the coming of the Spirit, as much as the Incarnation, is proclaimed by all the voices that ever spoke in the Name of God, as a mercy so great as to be an entirely new revelation of the manifold wisdom of God. How then shall we coordinate those overwhelming infinitudes? For let us be certain that there is coordination in them, that there is an order and a plan, as there is an order and a plan in a mountain range, though one mountain may seem to stand in the way of a higher mountain and intercept the view of the climber.

The fundamental realities of the spiritual life, then, are these: sanctifying grace, the three theological virtues, and the indwelling of the Three Persons of the Trinity. To these must be added, as a constant and everlasting adjunct, the seven gifts of the Spirit in their subjective reality, as vitalities inherent in the sanctified soul. The visible coming of the Spirit, which took place only once, as the Incarnation took place only once, appropriates first the seven gifts, and through them, the three theological virtues, in order to establish more completely the kingdom of the Three divine Persons, which is the ultimate purpose of all divine activity, which is the end of all the sacraments and of the Church and of everything that ever has been any activity or any movement in the world of the Spirit.

Visibility, experience, exteriority in one way or another, are the characteristics of the coming of the Spirit at Pentecost, in contradistinction to His invisible presence in virtue of the immutable nature of all created sanctification. God was made Flesh, God appeared as the Spirit of life, in order that man may be united with God in the very depths of his being. But in order to attain this end God leads man to God through the two supreme external manifestations of the Deity: the word made Flesh, the Spirit made into a sign. Christ gives us the divine plan in the following words: "I came forth from the Father and am come into the world: again I leave the world and I go to the Father" (John 16:28). So also the Spirit comes from the Father and the Son and manifests Himself in this world, in order to go back to the Father and the Son, not alone, but with us whom He has conquered; and the Father and the Son dwell in us.

It is of course to be admitted that right through the ages, the seven gifts of the Holy Ghost were operative, but never in the sense in which they are operative since Pentecost, because now we have not only a more intense stirring up of all that is in man through the Spirit, but we have a gathering together of all souls into one mighty society of the elect, the Church. Never before had the Spirit worked that work of creating the Church, of making the sons of God to be gathered into one. Sons of God there had been, but they were dispersed; Christ died in order to gather them together. Not only for one nation shall Jesus die: "But to gather together in one the children of God that were dispersed" (John 11:52). What Jesus did meritoriously through the power of His Blood, the Spirit does effectively through His Pentecostal presence all over the world to the end of times.

The newness and the originality of the work of the Holy Ghost at Pentecost is expressed in the idea of birth. It is said by the Fathers and Doctors that the Church was born on that day. The Bride dates her age from the fiftieth day after Christ's resurrection.

Many were the spiritual marvels that preceded this ever-blessed day; great things were done by the Son of God in His own Person; the family of God right through the ages had believed, had hoped, had loved, very often in a heroic degree, but the Church had not been born yet. It is simply and literally true to say that the mysterious reality of the supernatural order to which we give the name of Church was made then and has remained ever since and will endure for ever. In whatever way we look upon the action of the Spirit at Pentecost, this is its best definition: through it the Church was born. The whole faith had been given by Christ; the hierarchy had been established by Him; the sacraments had been instituted in their essentials; the principles of the supernatural life had been accepted, for Christ had not come to abolish anything, but to fulfill all things. Still, with all that, it is most exact to say that the Church was not born. It is as if a family were established for a long time, had great possessions, had a household full of splendor where every service was well carried out, but there was no heir yet. The birth of the heir will be considered as a day of paramount glory for that family. At Pentecost, then, the Holy Ghost added something essential, something substantial, to all that had been done by Him in the times past. He came and united Himself with that chosen portion of mankind called the Church, in a most manifest fashion: the baptism of the Spirit, as evident a distinction as had been the baptism of John, was bestowed on chosen men. In the days of the Precursor, men went about who gloried in the fact that they had been baptized by John; they were found all over the world. With the coming of the Spirit a new society sprang up, the society of those that were baptized in the Spirit, as the Lord foretold.

When we say that the Church was born on the day of Pentecost, we mean of course that the beginning of a life which is a total life, which is the whole new sanctity of Christianity, was started then; not only were external signs given of the presence of the Spirit, but an internal holiness, the holiness of the Church, began its mighty career on that day; it is the birth of Pentecostal holiness, a sanctity which has all the elements of the ancient godliness and much more. What that excess is, it is difficult to describe adequately; but no doubt the essence of the new holiness is this: the oneness of charity of all those that invoke the Name of Christ and constitute the Church. This is what St. Paul calls "drinking the same Spirit" (1 Cor 10:4). It is a profoundly social godliness, it is the "new commandment," the precept of mutual love which the Spirit with flaming power forces the disciples to obey: "A new commandment I give you, that you love each other as I have loved you" (John 13:34). It is the one heart and the one soul of the Christian community.

As we watch the apostles in their mode of life in the days that followed the pouring down of the Holy Ghost, we observe a double current of religion; they still keep the rites of the faith in which they had been brought up; they go up to the temple to pray as they had always done; they partake of the sacrifices as they had been accustomed from their childhood. But there is also the entirely new life, the new prayer, the new doctrine, the new rite of the "breaking of the bread," the new love, that makes the disciples give up their possessions; in fact, their religion is a new religion, it is not the old religion modified or made more perfect; it is the via nova, "the new way," in which Christians alone walk; it is the way of the Lord:

> Now a certain Jew, named Apollo, born at Alexandria, an elo-
> quent man, came to Ephesus, one mighty in the scriptures. This
> man was instructed in the way of the Lord: and being fervent
> in spirit, spoke and taught diligently the things that are of Jesus
> (Acts 18:24-25).

Very soon the Christians will entirely abandon the old way for the new, which conduct will mean their separation from the synagogue, their persecutions, their being sealed with the fiery mark of Christ in the furnace of tribulation.

In his first Epistle to the Corinthians, St. Paul, as we know, makes capital use of the great metaphor of the Body of Christ in order to bring home the necessity of Christian unity in spite of the diversity of gifts. This is for him an occasion of revealing to us the peculiar role of the Pentecostal Spirit in bringing about this exclusively Christian element: the oneness of all in one Body. It is through the Spirit that we are made one:

> But all these things, one and the same Spirit worketh, dividing
> to every one according as he will. For as the body is one and hath
> many members; and all the members of the body, whereas they
> are many, yet are one body: so also is Christ. For in one Spirit
> were we all baptized into one body, whether Jews or Gentiles,

whether bond or free: and in one Spirit we have all been made
to drink (1 Cor 12:11-13).

We are all plunged into one river of life, the Spirit; we all drink the
same cup of life, the Spirit; through the Spirit we are as one life. Such
unity never existed before: it is the miracle of Pentecost, a miracle
that will last through all eternity.

✠ 8 ✠

THE BRIDE'S WHITENESS

THERE IS NO THOUGHT MORE ANXIOUS FOR ANYONE TO whom the mystery of the Church is a constant subject for contemplation than the perils to which her innocence is exposed; the theology of the Church would be delightfully easy and most gloriously entrancing if all those who are her children were walking constantly in white garments, if the evil of mortal sin were not found among them. Above all, that very glory of the Church, that she is an extension of the mystery of the resurrection, seems to depend on her power to walk in the newness of life and to keep herself unspotted from the world. Were the angels of the resurrection not clad in white robes? Is not the whole atmosphere of Easter one of a greater innocence than even the innocence of childhood? So it is necessary for the Church in order to be the Spouse of a risen Christ to be one who walks with Him in the white garments of sinlessness.

We may make a distinction between the Church's sanctity and the Church's innocence. Sanctity is the abundance of the deeds of charity in the Church: innocence is the absence of sin, at least of deadly sin. It is round this matter of innocence that the great battle of sentiment is being fought. The Church is, and is called, a Bride; no wonder then that peculiar kinds of scandal are created in the minds of men when they see the stains of sin upon her. For so many, the wonderful and manifest fertility of the Church in every sort of good work is a spectacle for which they have no eyes; they pass it by as if it did not exist. On the other hand, sins real or imaginary, in the members of the Church, cause them to be scandalized in a way which is most evidently unhealthy; their scandal is almost pathological. Newman has castigated with fine irony that strange psychosis:

> So it is now; so it was twenty years ago; nay, so it has been in all years as they came, even the least controversial. If there was no call for a contest, at least there was the opportunity of a triumph. Who could want matter for a sermon, if ever his thoughts would not flow, whether for convenient digression, or effective peroration? Did a preacher wish for an illustration of heathen superstition or Jewish bigotry, or an instance of hypocrisy, ignorance or spiritual pride? the Catholics were at hand. The deliverance from Egypt, the golden calf, the fall of Dagon, the sin of Solomon, the cruelties of Jezabel, the worship of Baal, the destruction of the brazen serpent, the finding of the law, the captivity in Babylon, Nebuchodonosor's image, Pharisees, Sadducees, Herodians, and Zealots, mint, anise, and cummin, brazen pots and vessels, all in their respective places and ways, would give opportunity to a few grave words of allusion to the "monstrous errors" or the "childish absurdities" of the "Romish faith." Does anyone wish an example of pride? there stands Wolsey; of barbarity? there is the Duke of Alva; of rebellion? there is Becket; of ambition? there is Hil-

debrand; of profligacy? there is Caesar Borgia; of superstition? there is Louis the Eleventh; of fanaticism? there are the Crusaders. Saints and sinners, monks and laymen, the devout and the worldly, provided they be but Catholics, are heaped together in one indiscriminate mass, to be drawn forth for inspection and exposure according to the need (Wilfrid Ward, *Life of John Henry Cardinal Newman*, vol. 1. p.267).

How, then, are we to defend the innocence of the Church? We know of an instance in the Gospels when Christ undertook the defense of His disciples who had offended grievously in the eyes of the Pharisees. Passing through a cornfield they had plucked the ripe ears, had crushed them in their hands and had eaten them; and all this on the Sabbath day! The Pharisees were enraged over such a desecration; they trooped round the Master, accusing the disciples of this grave law-breaking, meaning, of course, to throw the whole blame on the One who was the leader of these men. Our Lord undertook the theological defense of His own in due form. He quoted the behavior of David when he ate the showbread; He mentioned the freedom of the priests in the temple on the Sabbath day; had they remembered, He concluded, all these things and more, they would not have condemned the innocent.

This expression, "the innocent," is a revelation of Christ's mind; He saw with absolute clearness what did matter and what did not matter in human behavior. May we not take it for granted that innumerable deeds done by Christians are declared innocent by the supreme Judge, however much they may scandalize men of ill will who are, openly or latently, the enemies of Christ? Censoriousness and fault-finding is the most common form of human evil-minded-ness; very little attention to our own motives will reveal the fact that we condemn certain acts and attitudes as evil simply because they are not our acts and our attitudes. The readiness not to think ill, which is one of the effects of charity, ought to be applied, not only to individual people, but before all things and above all things to that divine institution, the Church of Christ. It is not *parti pris* ("bias"), it is not a weakness of the too-eager apologist that should make us excuse the behavior of the Christian people as far as it is possible, it is simple charity. Too readily, perhaps, we accept without demur the whole complete charge against the Church made by an unkind world, as if Christians were the only sinners. It is as unwise as it is unjust thus to lend an ear to that great calumniator of the Church, the world. We should not be thus ready to believe evil in ordinary life. When St. Paul says of charity that it thinks no evil, he did not ask charity to be blind but only to be just.

We must always come back to the fundamental Christian measure of good and evil. In other portions of Catholic theology we never cease to repeat the golden axiom that sin is the only evil, and by sin we mean solely the free and deliberate revolt of the human will against the law of God. This way of assessing events ought to be applied to the Church's history with utmost exactness, and only those darknesses should be called evil which imply deliberate and grave disobedience on the part of the faithful against the law of Christ. Even where we speak of abuses we must remember this, that a so-called abuse could not stain the white robe of the Church unless the irregularity, of whatever nature, meant grave transgression of the law of God, either on the part of an individual Christian or on the part of groups of Christians. (Many a church historian has nothing but words of condemnation for certain church policies, certain methods of life, when after all, it would be difficult, not to say impossible, for the said historian to prove beyond doubt that the people who acted thus reprehensibly, according to his way of judging things, were committing sin habitually and were therefore in a state of spiritual enmity with God. The strongest condemnation of certain conditions in the Church, even uttered by saints, cannot be taken to be tantamount to a reprobation of the individual life of any Christian.

So much of the criticism of the Church's ways by her own sons, is concerned, not with absolute values, but with relative values. Those who embrace the more holy way are generally found not to be tender to such as follow the less holy way, though the weaker portion of Christ's people may be quite loyal to their Lord and even rich in merit. The one irremediable evil of the Church would be infidelity, the loss of belief. Apostasy from the faith is the supreme spiritual disorder: for that evil there is no compensation; it is unredeemed darkness.

The other evil we might describe as the sum of all the grievous sins—in the quite theological meaning of the word—which are committed by those who have the faith of Christ, and which, of course, in their full number and their complete bearing are known only to God.

But anyone who would gaze at that mountain of sin as a permanent indestructible incubus, crushing the Church, would be guilty of a grave error. Is not sin constantly being wiped away so that there is no trace of it in the heart of the men who committed it? Is not the power of penance a second baptism, giving back to the Church continually her original whiteness? To enumerate the sins of the Christian people and not to speak of their repentances is the conduct one generally ascribes to the spirit of darkness, Satan, who is called in the

Scriptures "the accuser of the brethren of the elect" (Rev 12:10), accusing them before the throne of God day and night. At the overthrow of that maligning spirit, of that denouncer of the faithful, the heavens rejoice. But an earthly accuser or rather objector, will say that most undeniably very often there existed in the Church conditions called abuses that made the life of the spirit a painful labor, that hampered the power of charity.

At present we are concerned, as already insinuated, mainly with the Church's whiteness, with her power to keep herself unspotted; this the Church can do and has done in spite of every kind of obstacle; she has truly been the lily among thorns; she has found it possible to avoid sin and to cleanse away guilt even when there was scandal. At no time has it been impossible for her to wash her robe in the Blood of the Lamb, because through her faith, which never suffered any diminution, she always stood in the very midst of the cleansing river of Christ's propitiatory power.

There is another glory possessed by the Bride: besides her white garment, she wears the raiment of gold, the positive acts of charity and sanctity. In this there is variety, there is abundance of wealth in a smaller or larger degree according to periods of greater or less fervor. Of this we shall speak elsewhere.

About one matter we must be careful; and to make us thus careful is the purpose of the present considerations. In fairness to the Church and in fairness to Christ we must not look at the Church through the sinful world in which she lives, that world for which Christ did not pray. We ought not to identify the Church with the world in which she has to exist; we must make a separation and even then when it can be said in perfect justice that the world has invaded the Church, we have to take cognizance of that continuous fight against worldliness which has never flagged and has been so conspicuous a feature of her life at various times. The Church's garment would truly have been stained had she finally accepted worldly standards in her practical conduct. This she never did, either in theory or in actuality; her stains are more like the cloud of dust that surrounds the traveler on the road where he has to journey in company with many others, it does not entail loss of purity, but it is a weariness of spirit.

When speaking of the Church's whiteness we do not mean, and we cannot mean, angelic whiteness; in accurate language we mean human whiteness, the purity that is possible to man whilst he dwells here on earth, whilst the soul inhabits a sinful body, a house of clay.

It is certain by all theological principles that no man here on earth can have the spotlessness of a spirit, the innocence of one who dwells in heaven. With the one exception of the Immaculate Mother of God, all Christians are in need of repentance for personal sin. It is precisely this uninterrupted presence of the spirit of repentance that makes the metaphor of whiteness a true metaphor in the case of the Church here on earth. Let us think of the Church's brilliancy as a white globe of light that dispels darkness; her garb is light, more truly than white linen; it is an active power, as the source of white light is an active power; it is not a dead surface but it is a constant renewal of brilliancy against the powers of darkness that would soon engulf her if she had not that interior fount of illumination, I mean her hatred of sin, her unceasing repentance for sin committed.

The classical passage in which the Church's innocence is described is in St. Paul's Epistle to the Ephesians:

> Christ also loved the church and delivered himself up for it: that he might sanctify it, cleansing it by the laver of water in the word

of life: that he might present it to himself, a glorious church, not having spot or wrinkle, or any such thing; but that it should be holy and without blemish (Eph 5:25-27).

It is to be admitted that St. Paul speaks of the Church here on earth. To the mind of the Apostle there was then only the Church with which he was constantly in contact, for which he worked, whose servant he was, over which the bishops were constituted to rule; she was not an abstract or distant Church. That whiteness and that youth are the whiteness and the youth of the Church at the present time. Christ has the power to bring it about. The unceasing operation of His grace obtains the result; the Church is not allowed to grow old, she is not allowed to have such spots as would really show a diseased body, she is without blemish. The Greek word here for blemish, *spilon*, may convey more than ordinary sin; it is a depravity that would be more like a corruption. Such a turpitude is never found in the Church; even then, when the Christian people commit many sins, their impurities are never such as not to be readily cleansed in the word of life.

The whiteness of the Church, in the words of St. Paul, is a whiteness obtained through the unceasing action of the Spouse of the Church, the action of sanctifying and cleansing. The fine linen, glittering and white, with which it is granted to the Church to cover herself is the justifications of the saints. Heaven itself, in a canticle of triumph, proclaims this truth. Justifications are active works, they are the constant endeavors of souls to pass from sin unto sanctity; the Greek term *dikaiōmata* means more particularly the amendment of wrong done:

And I heard as it were the voice of a great multitude, and as the voice of many waters, and as the voice of great thunders, saying:

Alleluia: for the Lord our God, the Almighty, hath reigned. Let us be glad and rejoice and give glory to him. For the marriage of the Lamb is come: and his wife hath prepared herself. And it is granted to her that she should clothe herself with fine linen, glittering and white. For the fine linen are the justifications of saints (Rev 19:6-8).

The difficulty which even Catholics experience in attributing to the Church here on earth great purity and sanctity may be met by a theological consideration which ought to have decisive power with anyone who is of the household of the faith. The reasoning is as follows. The purity and the sanctity of the heavenly Church are the reward of the Church's earthly life. Therefore in their substantial elements they must have existed in the Church in this world. No elect is admitted to the celestial kingdom unless he be found worthy of it at the moment of his death and therefore while still on this side of eternity. All essential purification and sanctification must be done in time, not in eternity. The Church is not washed in the Blood in heaven, but on earth. She works the deeds of charity while it is light, just as did her Spouse.

The reader will think naturally of the cleansing fire of Purgatory, a process that belongs to the other world. This is not the place to enter into the difficult problem of the role of the purifying of the soul as through fire, after death. It is not an essential purification, as it necessarily presupposes the whiteness of sanctifying grace, for only such are admitted to the abode of divine sorrow as have departed this life pure from all mortal sin. In exact theological thought it is true to say that, unless the terrestrial Church were pure and holy, the celestial Church could not be the glorious Bride she evidently is. These considerations are not so abstruse as not to be helpful in this great matter of the Bride's innocence.

It is to be remembered that the resurrection of Christ and the remission of sins are mysteries intimately connected. When Christ appeared to the disciples on the resurrection day He spoke thus to them:

> Receive ye the Holy Ghost. Whose sins you shall forgive, they
> are forgiven them: and whose sins you shall retain, they are re- ·
> tained (John 20:22-23).

The power of the resurrection is the power of forgiveness: the Church need not hesitate to approach her risen Lord. with Thomas she may put her finger into the place of the nails, she may put her hand into the side of Christ, for from that sacred Body there comes to her such cleansing that she will be quite at ease in the company of so holy a One as is the risen Christ.

✠ 9 ✠

THE BRIDE'S FAITH

I T CAN NEVER BE INSISTED UPON TOO FREQUENTLY THAT for the Catholic thinker the supreme and final ethical standards are the three theological virtues of faith, hope, and charity. Too readily in these modern times when the secularization of thought has made such terrific strides, do we accept other standards of perfection. Watchfulness in this matter of weights and measures in supernatural valuations is the duty of all preachers and writers on the things of God. It ought to be self-evident for Catholics that if the Church maintains in a high degree a life of faith, hope, and charity, her excellence as an institution remains unchallenged; above all, the Church will prove herself to be a most immediate radiation of Christ's glorification through those three qualities that are the very power of God, faith, hope, and charity. For truly through Christ's resurrection it has become possible for man to approach God more immediately in this threefold activity.

The three theological virtues, then, are the supreme manifestation of Christ's triumph, because through them man is sanctified in the midst of every possible and imaginable circumstance. St. Paul's wonderful challenge in the eighth chapter of the Epistle to the Romans is the sublimest canticle ever sung by man to express the glory of that faith and that hope which work through charity:

> Who shall accuse against the elect of God? God is he that justifieth: who is he that shall condemn? Christ Jesus that died: yea that is risen also again, who is at the right hand of God, who also maketh intercession for us. Who then shall separate us from the love of Christ? Shall tribulation? Or distress? Or famine? Or nakedness? Or danger? Or persecution? Or the sword? (As it is written: For thy sake, we are put to death all the day long. We are accounted as sheep for the slaughter.) But in all these things we overcome, because of him that hath loved us. For I am sure that neither death, nor life, nor angels, nor principalities, nor powers, nor things present, nor things to come, nor might, nor height, nor depth, nor any other creature, shall be able to separate us from the love of God which is in Christ Jesus our Lord (Rom 8:33-39).

In the present chapter we shall consider the Church's faith.

In the Canon of the Mass in the first of the three great prayers that precede the priest's communion, the celebrant addresses to Christ this supplication: "Look not upon my sins, but upon the faith of thy Church," *Ne respicias peccata mea, sed fidem Ecclesiae tuae*. The faith of the Church, if we are to believe the words of this solemn prayer, is a spectacle full of beauty for the eyes of Christ, that makes Him overlook the guilt of the individual Christian, nay, even of the individual priest. The faith of the Church indeed is the most marvelous of all spiritual phenomena known in this world. Its very existence as a corporate mental attitude of immense extent could not be explained but for the root mystery of the presence of the Spirit in the Bride. The Church's faith is an unalterable spiritual perfection; it has no vacillations, it has no succession of rise and fall, of peak points and diminutions, such as other spiritual qualities may show forth. It is always even, it is always serene, it never hesitates, never doubts; it is never obscure, it is never dormant; for the Church believes at all times, believes without intermission, and always believes the same things.

Those theologians then are right who consider faith to be the Church's body, the Church's flesh and bone, so that faith may be truly called the substance of the Church, her constitution, her stature and her size. It may not be possible for us to see at first sight how a spiritual quality and a mental attitude—faith is a spiritual quality and a mental attitude—could be the constitutional element of a society, nay, could be the society itself; for in ancient Christian language the terms faith and Church are synonymous; you belong to the Church because you share the great faith. But this is the triumphant achievement of the Spirit, of the God of truth, whose operations are supreme and irresistible: He maintains here on earth that wonderful thing—faith, and this He achieves independently of man's worth and man's sanctity. It is as if faith were a spiritual atmosphere that surrounds this planet and which those alone can breathe and inhale who are said to be "of the faith." This atmosphere has a divine purity and it remains uncontaminated; it rejects every kind of poisonous influence, and only such men move in it at ease who have received the gift of complete internal conformity with it.

This maintaining of the faith here on earth as a living reality gives the meaning of the presence of the Spirit in this world. This is the beauty of the Bride, this is her glory, that in a world of darkness and unbelief there should be this acceptance of the hidden mysteries of God, this love of truths which are hidden from the eyes of men, this tenacity not to swerve a hairsbreadth from the doctrine once revealed. Who can be the author of such a mentality, that has all the characteristics of a living personality? It is, of course, the Spirit, and the Bride is the mystical personality.

The first characteristic of the faith is this: that it is a vision of the unseen, a knowing of the unknown, a holding of the intangible, a love of the superhuman. Faith is essentially and from every point of view, transcendent: it is its very definition to be of the unseen, to be beyond the natural ken of the human intellect. Faith is not the aggregate sentiment of many men having the same interests; faith is not the voice of flesh and blood. It is not naturally in man to have faith in the Christian sense of the word. It is therefore necessary for us to visualize faith as possessing an existence by itself, independent of the merits of the men who profess it, having the Spirit to stand upon, as the surface of the earth is the solid basis on which there stand the greatest erections, the loftiest temples. This impersonality of the faith is of course an entirely new reality in human history, explainable only through the coming down of the Spirit of truth at Pentecost. Ever since that day there is on earth this beautifulness, this heavenly light, this resolve of will, this readiness to accept God's omnipotence, this splendor of vision. Faith is here on earth, not as a tyrant of the mind, but as an angel of the Lord, whose presence is an inexhaustible source of gladness. God sees this faith and He is appeased. God sees His own countenance reflected in faith and He abstains from destroying a sinful world.

For it is the world's only chance of finding grace before God that faith is still here on earth; if faith were to disappear there would be

no holding back the divine anger. But as long as there are human beings who believe what God has revealed unto them, who give glory
to God in accepting His word, however mysterious that word may
be, there is between this world and God a conformity, a similarity of
life; for no one could believe as the Christian is expected to believe
without God being greatly glorified. Faith is an acceptance of God's
truth that of necessity implies a great loyalty; no one can be a Christian without professing, at least implicitly, that God has the supreme
right of asking the allegiance of man's mind.

It is possible, of course, that the individual believer may be deficient
in charity, may be in a state of sin; that his faith, though sincere and
loyal, may be isolated from that part of his will which ought to be the
abode of the Holy Ghost; but this is a mere accident. Considered in
itself, faith is an unreserved good will towards God on the part of man.
The Church's faith, in the words of St. Thomas Aquinas, is full of that
beauty which he calls its "form," charity: *Fides ecclesiae est fides formata*,
"The faith of the Church is a formed faith" (*Summa*, II-II, q. 1, a. 9, ad
3). Individual believers may lack that special feature of beauty, namely
charity, but they move, none the less, in the atmosphere of faith, as men
move in an atmosphere indifferently whether it be cold or warm.

It is faith that constitutes the union of Christians amongst themselves; to be of the household of the faith is to be of the family of
God. It is not primarily charity that unites them; they are made into
one people initially through faith. To attempt a union through charity, without there being first unity of faith, would be as foolish as to
try to clothe with one and the same garment the disjointed members
of a body, separated by the axe of the executioner.

Faith is such that men can profess it externally, in all sincerity,
without any self-deception, without any illusion. A man knows when

he has faith. Countless members of the human race may profess the same faith, and their profession, beyond all cavil, makes them to be of one mind. Different is the nature of charity: it is more elusive; we are not certain of possessing it; we can deceive ourselves in many ways. It is not possible to make certain of a man's charity as it is possible to make certain of a man's faith. Faith is the house that gathers together the family of God; because it is indispensable that we should not mistake the house of anyone else for the house of God, and faith alone has that feature of being unmistakable.

It was the beginning of dangerous times for Christianity when men rose up and denounced the visibility of the faith as a useless phantom. Instead of the house of the faith they clamored for interior assurance, known to and perceived by the individual man only—the assurance that they were saved in Christ. This is, as everybody knows, the start of Lutheranism; it means an inversion of spiritual roles the magnitude of which only few people are able to understand. Each man walks in his own light, instead of there being the daylight of dogmatic Christianity in which the faithful move and have their being. To alter our metaphor, faith in the Catholic sense is the firmament above men's heads. The whole modern tendency, from Luther onwards, is to call "faith" what man feels within himself. It is, of course, evident that a faith which stands immutable on the face of the earth as an immense pillar of crystal—variety of metaphor in this rich matter is not a mixture of metaphors—is a very exacting power; it is truly that judgment of the world of which Christ speaks when He announces the coming of the Spirit of truth: "when he is come, he will convince the world of sin and of justice and of judgment" (John 16:8). Through such a faith the world is convicted of sin. A subjective faith may escape from this conviction, from this judgment of truth; it has a thousand ways of hiding itself, of wresting truth to its own perdition. The solid pillar of faith manifests the unworthiness not only of the unbeliever, but also of the believer, and more of the believer than of the unbeliever. The sinful believer is accused by the faith and rebuked by it, and there is no escaping from the sentence of a faith that is here on earth, not by man's grace, but through the omnipotence of the Spirit of truth. The sinful believer is found to be unworthy of the faith in which he dwells; the shame of his moral nakedness is seen by all people. He is the greater sinner because, in the light of the faith, his knowledge is more complete.

It is asked, is it not an unwise policy on the part of the Catholic Church to insist so much on the immutability of the articles of faith when it would seem that it is beyond the power of most men to live up to the heights of such a revelation? But here again we have to re-member the comforting mystery of the faith: it is not only a shining light but also a purifying fire, unceasingly eating away the impurities of the Christian soul. A faith that was nothing else than a manifesta-tion of sanctity would be quite intolerable for man. But a faith that is as much mercy as it is sanctity enables the Christian, in spite of all his sinfulness, to be a sincere believer without despairing, and above all, without being hypocritical. He can stand in the great light, he can make a profession of all these enormous and thrice-holy verities without blushing, though he may feel the guilt of his personal sin, because the very lintels of the house of the faith in which he dwells are dyed with the blood of the Son of God.

He stands where he stands because he has passed through the mystery of the death of the God of life, that death which is man's reconciliation with God.

✠ 10 ✠

The Bride's Hope

THE CHRISTIAN HOPE IS NOT THE SAME THING AS THE Christian faith. Very often we speak of faith and hope indiscriminately, as if belief in the unseen glories of Christianity were tantamount to possessing hope, to being endowed with the desire and with the will to stretch forth towards the prize of the heavenly vocation. It is evident, of course, that between the theological virtue of faith and the theological virtue of hope there is a close inter-relationship: only those can hope who believe; so there is little danger in an intermingling of concepts which does not discriminate accurately between faith and hope. Both virtues have this in common, that they survive in the Christian soul even when the Christian is not in charity. They can both be what theologians call "unformed," that is to say, they can exist in reality in man without the state of grace. It is possible, again, for someone to have faith and to lose hope; this would be the sin of despair, one of the most grievous sins which man can commit. Its most dreadful form would be this, that the Christian would believe all the verities of his faith, but that he would despair of his own salvation, of God's mercies towards himself individually. This is perhaps a rare sin, still it is a possible one.

Of hope we may speak, as we have spoken of faith, as being the glory of the Bride in the same sense in which faith is her glory. It is more than the accumulated hopes that are in the hearts of the faithful, it is the official attitude of the Church in this mighty problem—humanity's chances of laying hold on eternal life.

The hope of the Church as well as the faith of the Church, in the mind of St. Thomas Aquinas, is always informed, is never unformed: that is to say, the Church's hope is as that of one who is the friend of God, who is in the charity of God; that hope of the Bride has always the aroma of divine friendship, which, as we said, is not the invariable case with individual Christians. When we say that the Catholic Church possesses hope as the second great jewel in her diadem, we mean again a supernatural reality, far transcending the limits of an individual or of a number of individuals. Here once more we have to fall back on the fundamental constitutional principle of the Church, that special presence of the Holy Ghost which is the Church's unique privilege.

There exists, then, a body of feeling, a power of conviction here on earth that takes practically for granted this enormous fact, that God can be found by man, can be possessed by man, can be held by man eternally, in spite of the abysmal gulf that yawns between the infinite and the finite. For this is the meaning of theological hope, that through it we bridge over the chasm between the finite and the infinite, not in a speculative way only, but in a practical way; the finite rational creature ceases to hesitate in face of the infinite sanctity and from the depths of its lowliness it leaps forward and holds God, never to let Him depart. Hope is not a mere desire to find eternal happiness: such a wish could remain ineffective, a mere thirst for the impossible. Theological hope is the actual apprehending, by man's innermost possessive powers, of God in His own native purity of existence. Now the Church is the divine embodiment of that supernatural courage. It is the power of gravitation added to the solidity of the heavenly body. The faith of the Church, which is the solid body, is galvanized through and through with the mysterious activity of hope, that knows no obstacle in its path towards God. In hope the Church sings the triumphant words which her most heroic Apostle uttered for the first time, "I know whom I have believed and I am certain that he is able to keep that which I have committed unto him, against that day" (2 Tim 1:12), being a just judge.

What we may truly call the official hope of the Church is an overwhelming reality; there is simply no vestige of hesitation in any acts and movements of the Church concerning her power to obtain eternal life. This is manifested before all men through the Church's way of praying. Ecclesiastical prayer is the visible sign of the Church's hope; she hopes as she prays, and she prays as she hopes. Now of the Church's prayer there is no end; it is an unceasing stream, unfathomable in its depth, though all eyes can behold its surface. If the Church ceased to pray, her life of hope also would come to an end. But since the beginning, since the first Pentecost, there has never been any sign of fatigue. More truly than Moses on the mountain, the Bride is stretching forth her arms in supplication, and she is not in need of any supporters, as she knows of no lassitude, for the power of the Spirit is in her. The Church is truly the *Orans* of ancient iconography, the "praying" Bride. The supreme quality of the Church's prayer is that her trust remains unaffected by the multiplication of evil and sin amongst men. Nay, even her own losses and her own sufferings cast no cloud on the alacrity of her prayer, for she prays for those very people—her own and not her own—who fight against her, who buffet her, because through goodness she overcomes evil. The prayer of the Church is such that no individual man, however holy, could have thought it out first. Through the quality of the Church's prayer we see the truth of St. Paul's declaration:

> Likewise, the Spirit also helpeth our infirmity. For, we know not what we should pray for as we ought: but the Spirit himself asketh for us with unspeakable groanings. And he that searcheth the hearts knoweth what the Spirit desireth: because he asketh for the saints according to God (Rom 8:26-27).

Who can watch, without being profoundly moved, the life of the Catholic Church, from one end of the world to the other? It is an endless act of prayer, and in the midst of the greatest distresses there is never a word of despondency, never the remotest quiver of a doubt. She is sure that her prayer will be granted, that evil will be overcome, that the triumph of her Spouse will be manifest. Is it not a fact that outside the influence of the Catholic Church there is no such hope, and that man despairs of a higher order of things? The present calamity, the perplexity of the hour, the material solicitudes, have devoured him.

Quite publicly, before the eyes of the whole world, the Church declares it to be her chief business to save the souls of men. She speaks of that work of hers with truly astonishing realism, knowing full well that she can do what she has promised to do. There is no soul so debased as not to be the object of her maternal solicitude.

It is not without good reasons that we ought to renew our comprehension of this great claim of the Catholic Church of having the power to save souls. We are smothered with pseudo-salvationisms; the sacrosanct expression "to save souls" has been debased and emptied of all spiritual meaning by so many. The Christian notion of salvation is indeed replete with all the mysteries of good and evil, of heaven and hell. The Christian saint, who is full of the spirit of the Church, will declare with perfect sincerity that he is ready to lay down his life in order to bring about the salvation of one soul. Salvation of souls means a direct combat with all the powers of darkness; it means a fight with all the wild beasts of human passions; it means endless patience and heroic fortitude. It can be described by every kind of strong metaphor; it is a fighting with beasts, in the phrase of St. Paul, and it is a fishing of men, in the words of the Lord Himself. The obstacles that stand in the way of salvation are so great that no human similes will be completely serviceable.

Now it is this great work, this apparently hopeless task that is the Church's own work; it is her special craftsmanship, and in this she stands before all eyes as one endowed with unconquerable hope; for who could ever dream of saving the souls of men unless there were present in the bosom of such a one the double power of holding on to God and of holding on to man, as the rescuer of a drowning person will have his arm round the tree on the river's bank whilst the other arm lifts from the waters the unfortunate individual. For the Church does not only hold the conviction that man can be saved—this is part of her faith—but the Church saves through all the powers that are in her. She is a pioneer, she is a conqueror, she is wise in every enterprise, she lays deep and long plans and shows incredible readiness to make use of every opportunity to increase the number of the elect.

Here, again, we can pause and look with the eyes of our mind at this prodigious phenomenon, the Church's zeal, the Church's activity, in snatching souls from perdition and bringing them into the harbor of eternal salvation. For it is evident that this great war for the liberation of souls is not the war of individuals or groups of individuals, it is the war of the spiritual empire, the Church; it is not spasmodic fighting, nor is it merely self-defense; it is an endless campaign, and the temple of peace that will be opened at its termination is the temple of God that is in heaven. No earthly institution can show such a continuous plan of action, nor would human courage live so long.

There is in the Church's determination to save souls a very remarkable discarding of the element of time. Angels must be working thus; the vicissitudes of earthly durations hardly affect that activity of the Church. The institutions which she has built up for the salvation of souls are truly perennial. Of no soul does she ever despair: no sinner is abandoned by her; the greatest criminal, the most obstinate enemy of Christ, will have words of power of remission whispered into his ears to the last, even at the moment which is so near unto death that it is hardly distinguishable from it. So great is the hope of the Church, that the magnificent work of the justification of the ungodly, which, according to theologians is God's greatest achievement, comes quite natural to her; she takes it for granted that she can do it in the twinkling of an eye, if man gives her the remotest chance. She looks at the immense crowd of her enemies, not in terror, but in compassion, and says in as many words that many of them, if not most of them, will be saved ultimately from their own darkness by the might of her arm. The possibility of the conversion of the vilest of her persecutors is what one might truly call one of the Church's pet glories. There is a divine irony in this possible reversal of roles, when the persecutor will clamor on his death-bed for the ministrations of the Church of which he has spoken nothing but evil. The Church expects all that, is ready for all that, and she stands amongst us as the one power that never bends its knee to the Baal of human despair.

We might make a comparison between the Catholic doctrine of salvation and that conviction which quite accurately we might call the Lutheran conviction, whereby the individual man believes that he is saved in Christ. The latter is an isolated persuasion that may give or may not give peace and assurance to the man thus persuaded. The other is a victorious army on the march, a power of conquest, that spreads confidence wherever it plants its banner. The Catholic—and in this he is profoundly distinguished from the Lutheran—knows that the Church can save him and does save him; not only has he a personal confidence in Christ's redeeming power, but he has a direct participation in the Church's supremacy over all evil. The power of Christ has been communicated to the Church, the Spirit of love dwells in her; so for him the assurance that in Christ he will find salvation is not only a personal conviction, but is the certainty that he is surrounded on all sides by a victorious power, the Church. It is as if a child were lost in the darkness of a dense forest and a group of strong and friendly men came along, took him into their arms and carried him to his home; the child never doubted the love and the solicitude of his distant parents, but the advent of the band of rescuers changes his distress into joy. So the Christian soul, in Catholic mentality, is not only convinced of Christ's good will, it feels Christ's mighty arm through the ever-present Church, the rescuing Church, to whom no place is too dark, no wilderness too precipitous.

✠ 11 ✠

THE BRIDE'S CHARITY

I T IS AN AXIOMATIC POSITION MAINTAINED IN THIS BOOK that whilst there is immutability in the Church's faith, there is no such immutability in the Church's charity. It is our contention that the mysterious element called faith remains unalterable. Catholics always believe: if they lose their faith they no longer belong to the Church and their apostasy cannot affect the Church but only themselves.

Such is not the condition of that other mysterious element, charity, for many there are whose faith is genuine and sincere but who, through the state of mortal sin, are outside charity for periods more or less prolonged. In the days of fervor such cases get fewer and fewer; we should call that a period of prosperity when charity dwelt in the hearts of the believers to the extent of a hundred percent. Then again, charity has far more possibilities of progress than faith, as all merit comes from an increase of charity; higher sanctity is higher charity. Faith can also be progressive, but not in the measure in which charity can grow. In this power of progressiveness charity shows its superiority to faith: *major autem est caritas*, "for charity is greater." When there-fore we speak of the Church's charity, we are on less certain ground than we are with the virtue of hope and we do not possess those very clear issues which are peculiar to the Church's faith.

These reservations, however, are not meant to convey the impression that in the matter of charity the Church is not supreme, that the Bride of Christ has not the airs of a queen. Her charity is truly great-er than her faith and hope; through her charity she is the Bride of Christ and charity is the very blood of her heart. The doubt and the hesitation is not concerned with the immensity of the Church's char-ity or with the permanence of the Church's charity; the Bride's love could no more know interruption than her faith, because she would be a Bride no longer: that great fire burns unceasingly. But on account of its very excellence and intensity of action there are hearts among her own children that are not always aflame with it, because charity is a heavenly fire and many souls remain earthly though they be vessels that have the shape of the Christian faith. Powerful as the heat of the sun may be, unless the earthly body be turned towards it at a certain angle, the condition of the body will not be warmth but freezing point; the winter frost does not mean that the sun has ceased to send forth its rays of heat; the difference between summer and winter is a difference of angle in the earth's position. So there is in the charity of the Church an uninterrupted supremacy of power together with much indifference or coldness in many members of the Church; but at no time is charity diminished as far as the Church is concerned.

There is in the Church's official action a perfection of charity that marks her as the ever-faithful lover of Christ. Charity is this: to give God the preference in all things, even at the risk of losing all things; for this is supreme love that a man should lay down his life for his friend. Now it is evident that the Catholic Church has always shone through this resolve to give to Christ, not only the first, but the supreme place in all her thoughts. Nothing is more easily discerned than this attitude of unquestioning loyalty to the glory of the Son of God on the part of the Church. The Church, as Church, simply cannot have any other attitude than this of implicit surrender to God's claims, just as she cannot accept a doctrinal error.

When we say that the Church is infallible in faith and morals, by morals we mean this, that at no time could the Church, in her official capacity, act otherwise than in supreme charity. She could not teach any morality, any ethics, which would not be in perfect conformity with the charity of Christ. She could not make any concession to the world, she could not do the least act contrary to Christ's will in order to obtain temporal advantages. At all times the Church has preached that it is good for a man to lose everything rather than to offend Christ. She encourages, nay even enforces amongst such of her children as are capable of it, perfect renunciation. There is no sanctity so high as to be declared impossible by her; the word "impossible" does not exist for her in the sphere of love; all things are possible unto them that love Christ. Such has been most evidently the Church's practical judgment at all times and such it is today. Those states of perfection which are called the "evangelical counsels," are really charity at its best; never has the Church shown any change in her appreciation of them; she has always declared them to be feasible, and she surrounds with every kind of solicitude all those who profess that high degree of charity. In order to see what a real power the Church's charity is we need only think of what happened in that lamentable secession from the Church when Protestantism declared the vows of the Catholic religious to be useless, nay even unmoral. This is a palpable instance of the difference there is between the Bride of Christ and falsified Christianities. With all the power of assertion that is in her, the Catholic Church maintains that it is better for man to leave all things, that it is better for man to be a virgin, that it is better for man to give up his own will in order to possess Christ more fully.

It is a phenomenon as clear as daylight that right through the centuries the Church has never wavered in proclaiming God's supremacy in exacting from man an unquestioning obedience to God, in proclaiming the rights of Christ over mankind; in protesting against the vices of the world, in groaning over the sins of her own children, in working for the removal of all obstacles in the way of the Spirit. The whole mighty history of the Catholic Church is one great act of the love of God, because it is an unceasing proclamation of God's supreme rights. It is only a Church full of the love of God that could maintain the perennial fire of the Christian altar, I mean the Eucharistic holocaust, because through that great sacrifice God is perfectly glorified. Truly the Spirit is poured out over her, the Spirit of love, in which she cries, "Abba, Father." These great realities are maintained, not by an individual, nor by groups of individuals, but by one mysterious power called the Church, a power that never relaxes, a power that is always ready to avenge transgressions, a power that unceasingly pronounces the battle-cry, *Quis ut Deus?*, "Who is like unto God?" It is, in fact, conceded on all sides that the Catholic Church does maintain such a position most obstinately: it would even be said, most foolishly. She is suspected of suffering from illusions, from an other-worldliness which is tantamount to imbecility, in matters that concern the spiritual welfare of the human race.

In this proclamation of God's supremacy the Church has no rival. With a kind of sarcastic sneer the world leaves her to brandish the sword of the divine zeal; but the world, today more than ever, will tell the Church that she has found her match in the charity for man displayed in the world itself. The love of man, the brotherhood of man, the supremacy of mankind's welfare, have they not become the boast of our civilization? And the Church, whilst defending God, who after all ought to look after Himself, has forgotten to heal the wounds of humanity: another spirit has taken it up and philanthropy is certainly a competitor of ecclesiastical charity. Such indeed is the practical outlook of the world today. Can we really pretend that the works of charity of the Church, not towards God but towards man, reveal a divine power? It is, of course, beyond question that a civil state may do much for the well-being of its subjects, and that a whole period of civilization may be imbued with the special instinct of improving the temporal conditions of all men indiscriminately. Such a possibility is all the more likely to occur when the Christian religion for many centuries has proclaimed the ideals of the equality of all men before God; the secular power, thus urged on by the time-spirit, through all-round benevolence, will naturally have at its disposal material resources of very vast proportions; it will be able to achieve results in the betterment of human conditions which will be most imposing. But such achievements have nothing in common with Christian charity except the ideal that man is entitled to happiness in this life, an ideal which is originally Christian.

The love for man which is the human side of the theological virtue of charity must, of necessity, have for its object, not directly temporal happiness but spiritual happiness, the communication of eternal life. Such a pretension is, of course, derided by the world, and without any emulation the secular power leaves it to the Church to show her love of man in trying to save his soul. "I endure all things for the sake of the elect," says St. Paul, "that they may obtain the salvation which is in Christ Jesus" (2 Tim 2:10). The Apostle will be pitied by the philanthropist for he has at his disposal a much readier salvation, the salvation from material discomfort.

Thus then we are again confronted by a prodigious fact which is brought out through the contrast just established; in such a world as is our modern world, whose ideal is social service, the Church dares to maintain quite ostensibly the unpopular truth that man does not live by bread alone, that the greatest charity is shown to him when the word of God is preached to him, when his soul is justified and sanctified through the power of Christ. For this is the triumph of the Church's charity which our own generation more than any other is called upon to witness; when philanthropy has become the law of the world, the Church stands up and declares that he is a murderer who poisons the souls of men, who scandalizes the little ones that believe in Christ, who takes away from man his hope in a better life; he is a malefactor, though he were to fill the house of the poor with all the gold of the world. It was a comparatively easy position for the Church to show her immense superiority through her charity when human-ity was pagan outright, when man had not yet had time to adopt, as by contraband, certain Christian notions, but spoke quite frankly the language of human brutality as unregenerate humanity had always done before. Then it was charity versus barbarity, versus hardness of heart, versus slavery, versus tyranny. Nowadays, anyhow in the western States of Europe, charity stands out as the passionate lover of the soul versus the enemy of the soul, who declares himself to be the friend of man because he is full of solicitude for his temporal welfare.

For the Church to have remained as she has, so clearly conscious of the supreme spiritual values of eternal life and of the world to come, in a time of all-absorbing humanitarianism, is indeed to show forth a love of man that is tantamount to a divine genius. The Church's love has escaped the snares of the false lover, the evil spirit who gives to men all they want for their body if they fall down before him and adore him.

Far be it from us, moreover, to belittle the Church's corporeal charities, though in this matter, as said before, comparisons are expected to put her to shame. It is simply a fact that the Catholic people, in untold forms, practice unceasingly every sort of external bodily charity. The Church is in reality responsible for the existence in this world of the spirit of mercy, of the spirit of benignity, of the spirit of liberality. We may say with certainty that the Church's charity is complete even in this matter, though not all her individual members have always given the full measure of goodness towards their brethren: the Church's institutions have been as great in the alleviation of human misfortune as her physical powers permitted them to be at any given time. The Church lives quite naturally in the faith that whatever she does for man is done unto Christ Himself; no amount of human misery has been able to distract her from that simple perception. She knows that, were she but permitted to do it, this ideal of hers, this substitution of Christ for man in all the wounds of life, would alter the world's condition; she does not accept officially any other motive for every kind of beneficence. In this spirit she will look after the wounded of some terrible international war: in this spirit she will send her missionaries, her Sisters of Charity, to the lepers of the South Sea Islands; whatever she does, she does in the Name of the Lord Jesus, and her behavior, even when she goes into the dark alleys of human misery, is always the behavior of the Bride of the Son of God; she never heals the wounds of the body without giving back to man the consciousness of his own dignity. She comes as the elect of God, with the bowels of mercy, benignity, kindliness; but she never arrives without the power to cleanse the soul and produce in man's heart that happiness which the world cannot give even then when it gives food in abundance. The charity of the Church is not a spasmodic effort, is not a class preference, is not a condemnation of human conditions; it is the ennobling of man's body and man's soul under every sort of external condition.

✠ 12 ✠

THE CHURCH'S RENEWALS

A good deal of inaccurate and even misleading language is being constantly used with regard to one of the most mysterious phenomena in the supernatural order: the renovation of the life of the Catholic Church. By many it is taken for granted without any further investigation that periodically the Church comes near a state of exhaustion, that sins and abuses are multiplied to such a degree as actually to put the Church's life in danger; that Catholics become so tepid that they are on the brink of apostasy. From such alarming states the Church is, as periodically, saved by a divine intervention. This intervention is described in terms of an unexpected help from the outside, as if suddenly forces came into the Church that had not been there before. It is never said from whence those forces come, though the metaphors used by writers and speakers seem to indicate that they are from outside the Church, from some storehouse of energy whose location is, of course, never revealed. But the main impression is always that a new impulse is given to the Church from the outside, as if someone, some new spirit, some new system, some new idealism had arrived as a benevolent stranger with the message and the power of salvation. The one outside source of all salvation which is expressed in the dogmatic formula *Descendit de coelo*, "He came down from heaven," seems, in the minds of those people, to be an event that in minor degrees is often repeated.

Now nothing could be less in conformity with all we know of the constitution of the Church of Christ than this phantasm of outside helpers coming to the assistance of the Church at stated periods, bringing with them a life that was not there before. One might as well expect the human race to be rejuvenated and invigorated by blood from another planet. If there is one fact that is overwhelmingly clear in nature it is that mankind has in itself endless resources, not only to propagate but to renovate its own life, to repair all the damages caused by that state of society which we describe as decadence. Of course when we come to think of it, this power which humanity possesses is baffling beyond words. The race never goes beyond itself to renew itself. But what we see and admit in natural human family life we seem to miss in the supernatural family where tepidity, which is the counterpart of decadence, seems to us a fatal stagnation of life demanding to be balanced by vigor that comes from elsewhere, not from the family itself. Perhaps we are misled through the originality of certain great saints whom everybody admits to have been potent renewers of the Church but who, on account of their apparent differentiation of spiritual character, seem hardly to be the offspring of the life that went before them. So we are quite ready to speak of them as having been sent to the Church, like spirits from another sphere, to rouse the sleeping Peter from his slumbers. It is of course more poetical and in fact more easy to describe the Church's life and renovation as a succession of blows "striking Peter on the side" (Acts 12:7), than as an organic and ceaselessly developing life.

A little thought, then, will make us aware of the falseness, not to say the absurdity, of that facile and well-worn presentment of the Church's history. Let us station ourselves, so to speak, at any given period of the Church's career, at one of those epochs which by general consent are considered to have been golden days, seasons of life and vigor, times of fervor and sanctity. We may for instance fix our attention on those years which saw the emergence of the mendicant Orders, the advent of the Friars, with their tumultuous *joie de vivre* in Christ. They are, of course, only one of the many phenomena of a similar character, but they are perhaps the best known.

The first consideration that forces itself on any thinking mind is this, that such an army of enthusiasts could not be the offspring of a listless, faithless, tepid generation of Christians; they could not have come from a race of Catholics whose heart had grown cold, who had forgotten Christ. It would be against all biological laws, natural and supernatural, that absence of life should be succeeded immediately by abundance of life. The Friars in their fervor were the Christian people of their day, they were the sons of a Christian people through whom they learned everything that distinguished them, whose blood was in their veins, whose aspirations they merely carried further. Such a blossoming forth of the flowers of grace is only intelligible on the supposition that the soil was well prepared and ready for the breath of spring. It is not known in history that from an unbelieving people, an unspiritual race, there should spring forth all at once high sanctity on a large scale, except on the first pouring out of the Spirit; and even then the ground had been prepared by all the prophets, by the Precursor and by the greatest of the prophets, Christ Himself. So we may say in full confidence that any special generation of Christians distinguished by their sanctity is evidence of the sanctity that was before it. Saints are the children of saints.

It will be maintained that those renewals are truly something from the outside because the Spirit came and did work which He had not done before. Formulated in this wise, the objection betrays that very ignorance which has misled so many in this matter: ignorance concerning the Spirit's coming. The Holy Ghost, like the Word, came once: He does not come a second time; after His coming He abides, and it is this abiding presence that is the constant renewal of life; not a fresh advent like the one of the first Pentecost. The abiding Spirit prepares, in the souls of one generation of Christians, the spiritual life of the next generation of Christians, and so ad infinitum; but at no time does He abandon the Church in order to come back at a given moment in a whirlwind and in fire.

What blood is to the human race in the natural order, the Spirit is to the Church in the supernatural order; His potentialities are always present. Moreover not only the potentialities but the actual fruits of the Spirit in the souls of Christians are abundant beyond numbering at any given moment of the Church's history. If there were any interruption in the Church's spiritual fruitfulness, the gates of hell would have prevailed as truly as if there had been interruption in her faith, a contingency which to a Catholic is not even thinkable. The visible manifestations of fertility may differ, but it would be quite impossible for the Spirit to abide in the Church without there being some corresponding sanctity in the heart of the believer. Through its very definition, the abiding of the Spirit is not only a divine activity but a divine result, so that, once more through definition, if there were not created results of sanctity in the Church, the Spirit could on no account be said to remain in her. If there were no works of justice in the Christian people, the Spirit would as certainly have departed from the Church as the soul departs from the body at death, and a new coming of the Spirit, a new Pentecost, would be necessary. As a matter of fact there is nothing in history which in any way need make it difficult for us to accept without hesitation the view of the Church's uninterrupted sanctity. Wherever the historian turns he is met by innumerable monuments of active, genuine, often heroic, supernatural life. The three great functions of Christian sanctity, faith, hope, and charity, pulsate everywhere with undiminished vigor.

Most of my readers will have no difficulty in accepting this historic view, so full of optimism concerning the Catholic past, where the faith of our Catholic forefathers is concerned. It is mere tautology to say that the Church's faith is an unalterable function of her life, because without it she could not exist. Nor is there any difficulty concerning the theological hope of the whole Catholic past; if Christians in their millions had not hoped in God, had not expected from His mercies the gift of eternal life, the Church would have come to an end.

Where the optimism might seem misplaced is in the matter of the charity of the Catholicism of the bygone ages. Has there not been, by all accounts, a great cooling of the charity of the Christian peoples at various times? Are not their innumerable sins a terrible evidence of that diminution of charity? Have not those sins been at times so mountainous as to create the impression that all love for God and for man had gone out of the hearts of Christians? It is, of course, in this matter of charity and in this matter of charity only that we can speak of renewals inside the Church with any sense or meaning. But is there really any evidence forthcoming from the records of former generations that puts it beyond doubt that there have been periods since the first Pentecost when charity amongst Christians was dead, when their works of love had reached vanishing point, when they lived, universally almost, in a state of mortal sin?

The very statement of such an eventuality brings out the grotesqueness of the idea. Even at the periods which we might class as very sinful, with but little effort we shall discover beneath the unpromising surface innumerable and incontrovertible works of Christian charity. Moreover, to look at the sinfulness of the Christian people without remembering their constant and unceasing repentances, their confessions and their penances, is quite distinctly superficial naturalism. Much of the Church's sanctity is to be found in the sorrows and the tears of her sinful children for wrongs done to God and to man. Let us always bear in mind the truth enunciated elsewhere, that the sanctity of Christ's Bride here on earth is not the sanctity of angelic purity but the sanctity of loving repentance.

Shall we say then that there are no real renewals inside the Catholic Church, that much of modern eloquence on this matter has no rational foundation? Quite candidly, I think that by speaking so constantly of religious upheavals inside the Church, of religious revolutions, in the good sense of course, we betray ignorance of history as well as of theology. To my thinking, even the most astonishing changes and improvements that have taken place within the Church of God can easily be classed under the very authentic and theologically accurate notion of increase in faith, hope, and charity; for such an increase the Church prays, and whatever has happened in the days of triumph could never be more than a growth and an expansion of preexisting life. Increase in faith there may be both in intensity and extension, when the Christian people through the gifts of intelligence

and knowledge understand their faith better, write about it more elo-
quently, express it more artistically, when there is a great missionary
activity to establish faith in places where it was not heard of before.

Great also may be the progress of hope when Christians renounce
earthly possessions in more consider able numbers and with readier
alacrity.

As for charity, it is a consuming fire that at times may leap sky-
high, as the Spirit breathes on the flames. Here again let us remember
that the tears of repentance are also the effects of great charity. Charity may moreover multiply its ways, find new outlets, as it finds fresh
human miseries to heal.

But I do not think that there ever has happened in the Church
of God anything that cannot be adequately described in terms of an
increase of faith, hope, and charity. Now these holy realities were, of
course, never absent from the Church; they were never dormant, they
were not even at a low ebb. For this reason one finds it difficult to at-
tach a theological meaning to a term much used in modern history
books:—the term "Counter-Reformation." As it stands it implies an
upheaval in the good sense inside the Church, as outside the Church,
through the falling away of so many at the Reformation, there was
an upheaval in the evil sense. It would be positively absurd to maintain that in her own life the Roman Church has, at any time, to do
catastrophic things in order to bring about spiritual health and supernatural equilibrium. The Church did then what she had done often before and what she did in the days after the so-called Counter-
Reformation: she fought sin in all its ramifications.

There could never have been that glorious manifestation of faith,
hope, and charity of which the latter half of the sixteenth century
gives us the spectacle if, in its earlier decades, there had not been

abundance of those same divine qualities. For, after all, the Christians of that second portion of the century were the children of the Christians of the first half of it. The splendid defenders of the faith, the brilliant theologians of the period of the Council of Trent, were men formed in the Catholic schools that were the institutions of the pre-reformation Church. Nothing could be more suggestive and help us more potently to understand the continuousness of ecclesiastical life than to observe how the battle against the sixteenth-century heresies was fought exclusively with the weapons of the long-established theology.

✠ 13 ✠

The Beauty of the Pentecostal Spirit

S<small>T.</small> P<small>ETER</small>, <small>IN HIS FIRST</small> E<small>PISTLE</small>, <small>DESCRIBES IN THE</small> following terms the Christian's relationship with Christ, "whom having not seen, you love: in whom also now, though you see him not, you believe and, believing, shall rejoice with joy unspeakable and glorified" (1 Pet 1:8). Of the Spirit he says in the same passage. "The Holy Ghost being sent down from heaven, on whom the angels desire to look" (1 Pet 1:12). The Christ is hidden in the heavens but the Spirit is sent from heaven, and the Spirit, thus sent, is not a Spirit in a state of humiliation but the Spirit in His full glory: He is the Spirit "on whom the angels desire to look."

The coming of the Holy Ghost at Pentecost never leaves the mind of Peter; his descriptions of that sweet Spirit in this Epistle, written so many years after the event, is as beautiful as it is unexpected: the angels desire to look on that Spirit. He is therefore One who is full of beauty, He is One who fulfills the cravings of man, but who, bringing satisfaction to man's desires, kindles them with a further craving.

The mighty angelic choirs are also animated by the Holy Ghost;

He is the bond of union between choir and choir, between hierarchy and hierarchy, in the kingdom of glory: those mighty intelligences find in the Spirit their common center. What is the role of the Holy Ghost amongst the angels of God in heaven? The words of St. Peter certainly convey the idea that in some wonderful manner He is their particular glory. We must always remember that the existence of those holy beings is conditioned by their finiteness; none of them is infinite; therefore they are in need of the supernatural order, they are in need of the Holy Ghost, as man here on earth is in need of Him. The thought should give us endless joy, that the Spirit who fills with His breathings this immense angelic world, is also our Spirit.

The greatness and exaltation of our Christian life could hardly be stated in terms more astonishing than the words of Peter: "The Holy Ghost being sent down from heaven, on whom the angels desire to look." Is this not a revelation on the part of Peter of what he knew and felt on the great day of Pentecost? Hardly anything is said, as we know, of the interior experience of those holy men on that occasion. How was each one of them affected in the depth of his soul in that moment? Holy writ just says that they were filled with the Holy Ghost, but how long did they remain in a state of passivity under that mighty inrush? No doubt it influenced each one of them in some peculiar and personal way. With wonder we ask the question, what were then the sensations of the ever-blessed Mother of God? It was her second great communion with the Spirit: the first time the Holy Ghost had come down upon her when she conceived in the womb the Son of God. Now there was this crowning exhilaration of her heart in the Spirit. Shall we not conclude from St. Peter's charming phrase that he was made conscious of an intimate association with the heavenly spirits in that hour of illumination? That he knew himself to be transformed by the same Spirit that makes of the heavenly hierarchies one mighty army of love? It would be—one might venture this remark—in keeping with Peter's special position; he being at the head of the earthly hierarchy would be granted in an unusual way the understanding of that great unity which makes of all the elect, angels and men, one complete, mystical Body of Christ.

This drinking of one Spirit makes us all into brethren. Christian life, therefore, has been called the angelic life with perfect exactness of language. Such an expression is not demanding too much of us. Far from us to pretend that the mortal conditions of man are angelic conditions; this would be a sad illusion; we have the burden of our flesh and blood, we have the temptations and tribulations of the time of trial. But we are angelic through the Holy Ghost, because one and the same Spirit vivifies all of us, from the simplest Christian on earth to the Cherub before the throne of God.

This is our true supernatural quality: there could be no greater community than this. All other gifts, even the gifts of grace, are modified by the vessel that receives them. An angelic spirit has sanctifying grace in a fashion that is conformable to his lofty nature. Not so with the gift of the Spirit Himself because the Spirit is not received according to the shape of the recipient, but He is received unmodified: it is God and nothing but God.

Was it not this vision that made Peter say in praise of the Spirit that the angels desire to look upon Him? He is greater than they are, He is greater than their grace. In going out to Him, in gazing upon Him, they find their union with Him. He is to them what He is to us; He is to us what He is to them: a reality of transcending beauty and power.

This characteristic of the Spirit, to be in us and yet to be above us, is manifested in the Church here on earth. There is always a power that transcends all the graces and all the gifts of individual Christians. The highest endowments of the souls of the redeemed are after all personal endowments, they are part and parcel of the individual, they may be very broad and very high, but they are always personal, they are never universal. Now it is a fact that the Church has a spirit which is always greater than the accumulated spirits of her children: the Holy Ghost, whose rulings can never be deflected by the individual saint. What saint or what class of saints could pretend that they are the full expression of the mystery of Christ or of the will of God? Peter will differ from Paul, John will differ from Paul and Peter, though they be all three giants in charity. But there is one uniformity before which everybody yields: the uniformity of the Spirit.

The Church can truly say "it has seemed good to us and to the Holy Ghost" (Acts 15:28), as she speaks in the Acts of the Apostles. This is indeed an astonishing claim, but it is Catholicism; it makes all individual thought and interest, however perfect, subservient to one supreme thought which is never deflected from the high plane of universal truthfulness, the Holy Ghost. This is the origin of the fine Christian manner which makes us speak humbly of even our greatest virtues, which makes us ready to bring our operations, however lofty in their aim, into conformity with something higher, the will of the Spirit. We are not sad at relinquishing our own works because the Spirit has a higher plan.

St. Peter himself is a beautiful instance of this surrender to the Spirit. It is in his dealings with the first heathens, Cornelius and his household, that we see him at his best as the true "Son of the Dove," for such is the name which the Fathers liked to give to the Prince of the Apostles:

And when I had begun to speak, the Holy Ghost fell upon them, as upon us also in the beginning. And I remembered the word of the Lord, how that he said: John indeed   with water, but you shall be baptized with the Holy Ghost. If then God gave them the same grace, as to us also who believed in the Lord Jesus Christ: who was I, that could withstand God (Acts 11:15-17)?

These last words, "who was I, that could withstand God?" are Peter through and through; his own gifts, his own work, what are they? He feels like one who is nothing in the presence of that supreme element, the Holy Ghost, who is poured out alike on Jew and Gentile, on man and angel, who takes earth up to heaven and brings heaven down to earth again.

There is in the supernatural world a distinction that can never be lost sight of if we are to understand what is meant by the Spirit whom the angels crave to behold. It is the distinction between Spirit and spirits; by spirits we mean the rational minds, sanctified in ways innumerable; it is the variety of the Bride of Christ, *circumdata varietate,* "surrounded by variety." Those differences are made up through nature and through grace; rational creatures differ profoundly even in sanctity; all their graces and endowments are gifts and they are consequently subjective possessions. We should even say they are the gift of the Spirit, the Holy Ghost, as with the Father and the Son He shapes the vessels of election.

In this sense we speak of a spirit as informing at times whole generations of Christians or whole groups of Christians; in this meaning we can speak of the spirit of a religious Order; it means the possession of a certain gift of grace by many. It could be said that the spirit changes and such a change need not be taken in evil part, as new needs may require new powers. In our own time more than ever we are interested in this variety of gift, in this diversity of spirit; we analyze the spirit lovingly, we examine all its facets. But what should we say if we could behold the varieties of the angelic spirits, the diversities of powers, the degrees of will and intellect, the endless multiplicity of graces?

The Spirit who is sent from heaven is one because He is infinite. He makes use of all the gifts which He Himself has imparted, as if a great artist played on a variety of instruments which he himself had thought out and made with his own hands. The oneness of the Church is the manifest sign of that Spirit who transcends all spirits. It would not be possible for the Church to possess unity if the divine Spirit were not present, as the variety of created spirits would lead to dissension rather than to conformity; for the more powerful the spirit, the more assertive it would be, to the detriment of the harmony of peace.

It may be a charming study and a most edifying one to enter into the workings of the spirit of the saints; we may speak of it as renewals of the face of the earth, as powers that save the Church at a given moment; but when we look thus at the army of Christians, in the varied panoply of the supernatural armor, fighting each one bravely according to the spirit that is in him, let us not forget that above all the scintillating array of the spiritual weapons there is a weapon which is not put into the hands of any man, the weapon of the Spirit Himself. All the enthusiasms of the soldiers of Christ would lead them into varieties of opposite actions unless they were captained by the Spirit who knows all spirits, who holds all things in His hands, and who alone has unlimited vision and infinite power.

✠ 14 ✠

THE PERMANENT GLORIES
OF THE BRIDE

THERE IS IN THE HISTORY OF CHRISTIAN RELIGION
a purism that is laudable, and there is a purism that is dangerous. The term "puritanism" has been definitely given over to a manifestation of that Protestant spirit whose works are chiefly the discarding of certain forms of external religion, nay, even the destruction of
its material emblems. Purism is a much vaster attitude and *a priori* it
is a desirable religious phenomenon inside Christianity; we describe
as "purism" that attitude of mind which asks for a Christianity that
has no human accretions.

Faith is always called pure when it is orthodox and traditional;
the word purity seems to belong to it by a kind of birthright, *fides
pura* "pure faith" is an expression that goes right back to the Apostles.
The idea seems to be that faith has walked for so many centuries the
dusty road of human history and has kept her garment white. A "corrupt faith," *fides corrupta*, is the sad possession of those whose mind
has been troubled by error and who have left the Church to follow
their own thoughts. Christian language is more inclined to use the

term "corruption" in connection with the doctrinal attitude of men than with their moral attitude; only in more recent times has the word "corruption" been applied with a moral significance. It is the Protestant accusation against the Catholic Church that she has been corrupt or is corrupt on account of much sinfulness and abuse found in her members. The older Christian generations would have called corruption a doctrinal perversion, a departure from tradition. It is in this sense of doctrinal purism that we speak of purism here.

We say that the Church is pure if she possesses today the faith of the apostolic age. But in this matter there is variety as well as purism; faith, being essentially an element of life, could not remain monotonous, it could not be considered in the light of an heirloom which remains unaffected by the tastes of succeeding generations. The manner of expressing the faith has great variety, and it would be a dangerous purism that were to insist on an absolutely unalterable form of expression. Such purism would be archaism and it might lead to puritanism, to a heresy.

The mode in which faith is expressed is what we might call the human side of Christianity; it is in fact the only kind of human side of which we can speak with any sense in this matter of religion. We should not describe the sinfulness of religious people, their imperfections and passions, as the human side of religion; these things are simply the shortcomings of man though he be raised to the supernatural order. When we use the expression "the human side of religion," we are really thinking of something entirely laudable, of something that comes from the Spirit, of something that is the glory of the Bride. It is this: as the human race is not a stable, unchanging factor but one that alters and progresses according to laws of life, faith itself—we mean that divine faith which is the Church's very substance—takes a different hue, acts differently, feels differently, works differently; and that variety, far from being a loss of purity is an emblem of purity, because no life is more adaptable to environment than a pure life, a strong life, an uncontaminated life. It is the proper quality of youth and strength to be responsive to new factors of life; old age and decay are hard and irresponsive.

It is consequently the perpetual boast of the Catholic Church that her faith is as pure today as it ever was, and that her people are completely apostolic in their religion; that they are the immediate brethren of the early Christians, though in so many ways they express their faith differently from what we know to have been the manners of the Christians in earlier centuries.

Nothing would be easier than to write the history of those variations. An artist would be the best person to do this great matter justice, for, to a large extent, the varieties are of the aesthetic order. But other elements besides the artistic element have played a great role in producing the Catholic variety; we might use the word temperament as being perhaps the most accurate for a phenomenon so prodigious. It is a wise rule in this vast subject not to condemn any fashion which the faith may have assumed at a special time. Every generation of Christians has a new spiritual temperament, and the Holy Ghost has the knowledge of all those moods of the human spirit because He is the maker of man. His great praise in the Pentecostal liturgy is this: *Hoc quod continet omnia scientiam habet vocis*, "He that holds everything in His hand has the knowledge of every speech." He knows how the heart of man beats at various times.

That temperament is caused by mankind's life, by the struggles, by the wars, by the discoveries, by the progress in art and science, and not least by the manifestation of evil that always surrounds the

Church because the Prince of this world is the great adversary of the Church. One generation of Christians may feel in a repentant mood more for the sins of the previous generation than for their own guilt, whilst another generation may be keenly aware of the iniquities of the world outside itself. There is no limit to the sources of the variety of temperament in the Christian people.

My contention here is this: that the proportion between the permanent and unalterable life of the Church and what we might call her temperamental life is as a thousand to one; that is to say, when everything is considered, and wonderful as the variety aspect is admitted to be, the immensely greater wonder is the unchangeableness of the faith in all its aspects. The Christians of today may differ from the Christians of the second century but the differences are hardly more than, say, the varieties of a dialect within the language spoken in the various provinces of the same country. It is possible that we may pay more attention to the difference than to the identity; such is the human mind, it seizes on differences because they are a phenomenon in opposition to the monotonous substance.

Let us put the matter into a well-known form: there is, for instance, much talk concerning the variety in spirit in saints, in founders of Orders, how one religious family is said to meet the needs of a special period, in preference to another religious family. All this we grant ungrudgingly; but if we come to look at the matter more closely what do we find? A new gospel? a new doctrine? a new ascetism? a new sacrament? a new spirit? a new revelation? Of course none of these things are new. So great is the *depositum fidei*, "the deposit of faith", so great are the demands of the permanent duties of the Christian soul, that the so-called new spirit can hardly be anything else than a slight difference in the way of carrying the glorious ancient burden. What is the so-called new spirit, for instance, compared with the contents of the Eucharistic faith, a faith that is essentially unalterable?

We may put the matter again in this wise: two men, fervent servants of Christ, will be described as belonging to two different schools of spirituality; perhaps they are members of two different religious orders. In modern parlance they will be spoken of as two distinct types of religious life inside the Church. Here again we readily grant differentiations, but what are those dissimilarities if we come to enumerate, even in a summary fashion, the living matters of their faith that are common to them both? The two men are full of the faith in One God in Three Persons; they admit that God became man; the death and the resurrection of the Son of God they hold by common consent; they believe in eternal life in a state of incomprehensible glory; being priests they celebrate every day the sacrifice of Mass. And so we might go on enumerating all they do in common, all they believe in common, all they love in common. All the principles of the spiritual life are common to them both because charity, which is the bond of perfection, admits of no difference. Truly when we reflect on this prodigious oneness in God we must wonder why the differences have made such an impression on men's minds.

There are in the Scriptures many allusions to differences of gifts and of graces, but these are not what we call, in modern phraseology, the particular spirit of a given set of religious men or women. The different graces of the Spirit, in apostolic language, are permanent values. They are not granted to all men at all times, but when they are granted they establish a great similarity between the people thus endowed; as if, for instance, two chosen Christians were both endowed with the gift of prophecy, such types of perfection would be alike in whatever century of the Church's life they might be found.

This is perhaps the place where we might say something on the value and meaning of controversies in spiritual matters inside the Church. It is evident that very great differences exist in the minds of theologians and also in the minds of mystical writers concerning various points. Theological controversies are famous for the passions which at times they have aroused; likewise men have taken up vehemently either one side or the other in speculations concerning the nature of the mystical life. The tomes that are filled with those debates are an imposing array of learning. Non-Catholics who are unused to the freedom of the Catholic mind are sometimes scandalized by those dissensions of the learned. They will even say that oneness of faith does not exist in reality inside the Catholic Church, as there is so much discord in the sphere of speculative theology. It is quite true that whole centuries resounded with theological debates, that immense talent was thrown into the fray, that it appeared at times as if the very foundations of Catholic thought were being shaken; the ardor of the argumentations could hardly have been fiercer when orthodoxy fought heresy in earnest.

But a moment's sober survey of that noisy battle will reveal the fact that the debated points are like a few stones that are detached by the thaw of spring from the mountain side and rush down the slope with great noise; the mountain itself remains unmoved. Theological debates are to accepted faith what a loose pebble is to a mountain range. We play with the pebble, hence our animosities; but we do not play with the mountain.

Thus, what are differences concerning, say, the mode in which the Eucharistic mystery is a sacrifice, compared with the mountainous dogmatic fact, which every Catholic accepts, of transubstantiation itself? Men who believe in transubstantiation can afford to differ in much else before their oneness of mind suffers; for many minds to accept a dogma of that size is indeed a unity of faith so great that other differences do not count. Behind our controversies there is such a massive acceptance of truths, great beyond comprehension, that the most fervid turmoil concerning the mode of explaining this dogma or that is hardly a ripple on the surface of the Catholic mind.

When Arius declared that the Son of God was less than the Father, in fact was a creature, the Church knew instinctively that something catastrophic was threatened: it was not an opinion, it was a dogmatic landslide: it was the difference between the finite and the infinite in the Church's spiritual wealth. When Nestorius divided the God made Man into two distinct persons, he surrendered Christianity wholesale, because in such a theory it was no longer true to say that God had died for man. When Pelagius denied grace, he denied life, as the Church understands life. When Luther denounced Mass as an idle ceremony, the very essence of Catholicism was at stake.

Heresies—and such things were heresies—are each one a yawning abyss ready to swallow up the army of God. The acutest controversies amongst Catholic theologians concerning grace, the modes of Hypostatic Union, the ways in which the Eucharistic mystery is a sacrifice, are exercises of the intellectual militia of the Church, carried out far from the edge of the great abyss of heresy. It would indeed be a very sad misreading of the history of the Church if we gave those animated debates of theological schools a preponderant place in the description of the Church's life.

The unceasing celebration of the Church's liturgy in which the eternal truths are being constantly reasserted with ever increasing solemnity is, of course, a spiritual phenomenon so vast that it defies description; but it is the normal life of the people of God and therefore is not the object of the historiographer but the spectacle which the angels of God love to behold, for it is truly eternal life on earth.

✠ 15 ✠

THE SEVENFOLD SPIRIT

THE CONSIDERATIONS OF THE PREVIOUS CHAPTERS prepare us for the wholehearted acceptance of an axiom of Catholic theology which is the guiding principle in the doctrine of the seven gifts of the Holy Ghost. In all the varieties of the heavenly endowments which make of man and of angels the children of God, there is a set of perfections which are called specifically the seven gifts of the Holy Ghost, and on account of them the Spirit Himself is not infrequently called the Sevenfold Spirit. Those seven powers are enumerated for the first time by the prophet Isaiah when he gives an anticipatory portrait of the All-Beautiful, of the Flower of creation, Jesus Christ:

> And there shall come forth a rod out of the root of Jesse: and a flower shall rise up out of his root. And the spirit of the Lord shall rest upon him: the spirit of wisdom and of understanding, the spirit of counsel and of fortitude, the spirit of knowledge and of godliness. And he shall be filled with the spirit of the fear of

the Lord. He shall not judge according to the sight of the eyes, nor reprove according to the hearing of the ears (Isa 11:1-3).

The prophet here is speaking of the human nature of the Son of God, but the gifts he mentions are universal gifts, which are possessed by the brethren of Christ here on earth and by the angels of God in heaven. The seven powers are not the Holy Ghost Himself in His Person, but they are a variety of subjective gifts which are His special, chosen instruments.

In this matter Catholic theology has always shown great wisdom: it has never made the mistake of identifying the seven gifts of the Holy Ghost with the Holy Ghost Himself. Even in the sevenfold spirituality that division of which we spoke in a previous chapter exists, the division between the Spirit and the spirits. The Christian has seven spirits, that is to say, seven different spiritual qualities, but he has only one Spirit who guides him.

The seven gifts of the Holy Ghost, then, are seven various qualities entirely subjective, that reside in the souls which possess charity. They not only make the Christian conformable to the Holy Ghost, but they make him into a being ready at any moment to be moved by the Spirit that comes down from heaven, whom the angels desire to contemplate. It is, I said, an extremely prudent thing on the part of Catholic theology to have maintained in this matter of the gifts of the Holy Ghost the distinction between the Person of the Holy Ghost and those wonderful dispositions which are rooted in human personalities. It would seem that unless we have a Spirit who is absolutely transcending, that unity of souls, which is the Christian Church in her perfection, could not be attained. Most of our spiritual endowments would still be centrifugal, because they are the possession of an independent, finite individual. So the gifts of the Holy Ghost are described as so many dispositions which make man easily centripetal, provided the one transcending Spirit breathes on them, as a powerful wind may move all vessels in one direction.

The scholastic theologian says that through the seven gifts of the Holy Ghost the creature becomes *facile mobile*, "easily moveable" by the Spirit, without being anchored to this human interest or that, to this human view or to that. The danger is self-centeredness, complacency in our own riches. Among our gifts, then, there are qualities designed directly for this purpose, to turn everything that is in us, however holy, away from us unto God; the seven gifts fulfill that function. But even then the Spirit Himself must lift man above himself, for the consummation of all the works of God is this, that from himself man passes into God, so that God be all in all. This then is the peculiar feature of the seven gifts of the Holy Ghost, that through them the Church first and then individual souls are directly in contact with Divinity itself. It is the creature's divinization.

It is, of course, possible for individual man to extinguish the Spirit, it is possible for him to withdraw himself from the influences of that divine breath; but when he walks by the Spirit, when he surrenders himself to the divine motion, he has truly become the heir of the kingdom of heaven.

In Catholic theology we should consider the fall of the angels in this light of a refusal to follow the Spirit. Those wonderful creatures whom God made first, were full of every beauty, replete with every supernatural quality; they could not sin through any passion; their only danger was this, that they should take complacency in themselves, in their own gifts, even in their supernatural powers through no longer surrendering themselves to a will that was outside themselves, the motion of the Spirit. Angelic sin would be essentially a sin against the Holy Ghost, a refusal to go there where the Spirit leads.

Through the seven gifts, then, the Church here on earth is saved over and over again from this danger of making this world the end of all her efforts, of being satisfied with human achievement, with temporal glory.

Let us consider the position of the Church, placed amongst men with all her excellencies. That she should not please man but God in all things she owes to the operation of the seven gifts. If Christianity ever sank to the level of a perfect ethical society whose sole aim it would be to further temporal prosperity, nay, even temporal honesty of life, the Church would have as truly apostatized as Lucifer himself: she would have denied the Spirit, she would have refused to follow Him where He wants her to go; she would please man instead of pleasing Christ, she would make the applause of mankind her supreme reward. The Church has been rescued from so great a catastrophe in spite of all the dangers that have beset her course.

To become worldly is a peril that is never absent; when we say that worldliness is her snare we mean by worldliness a more subtle thing than is usually meant by this expression. We generally understand by worldliness the love of wealth and luxury amongst the Church's dignitaries; this is, of course, an evil, but it is not the principal evil. Worldliness of the mind, if it were ever to overtake her, would be much more disastrous for the Church than worldliness of apparel. By worldliness of mind we understand the practical relinquishing of other-worldliness, so that moral and even spiritual standards should be based, not on what is the glory of the Lord, but on what is the profit of man: an entirely anthropocentric outlook would be exactly what we mean by worldliness. Even if men were filled with every spiritual perfection, but if such perfections were not referred to God (suppose this hypothesis to be possible), it would be unredeemed worldliness.

Now from this evil, as we said, the Spirit saves the Church through the seven gifts. This is why we speak of these gifts as being non-ethical, or rather supra-ethical, because they create, in the Church and in individual souls, attitudes that cannot be classified under any ethical system. We consider therefore that the eight beatitudes of the Gospel are the practical expression in the Church of the seven gifts of the Holy Ghost, because in the eight beatitudes a behavior is described for Christians that has no foundation in ordinary morality. We should not say that there is opposition between philosophical ethics and the eight beatitudes; they are not in opposition, but they do not belong to one and the same sphere of goodness. The poor in spirit, the meek, the mourner, the man who hungers and thirsts after justice, the merciful, the clean of heart, the peacemaker, the sufferer under persecution for justice's sake, the one who is reviled—all these are types of another world; and though in some aspects the qualities of the beatitudes seem to come near to certain natural ethical perfections, in their full bearing they are as much above man's rational goodness as heaven is above the earth. They are the morality of an entirely new world, the world of God. They are a happiness in the supposition only that it has pleased God to give a wholly new kingdom to the little flock:

> Be glad and rejoice, for your reward is very great in heaven. For so they persecuted the prophets that were before you (Matt 5:12).

It is evident that the beatitudes would be diametrically opposed to the instincts of a Church that is completely anthropocentric in the sense we have described. The permanence of the eight beatitudes in the Church, as the officially and universally recognized code of sanctity, is indeed a phenomenon of incalculable meaning.

A very clear instance of the abandonment of the Spirit would be found in the element of nationalism if it were allowed to shape the Church completely and logically. Nationalism was the first experience Christians had in the way of opposition when the Jewish race refused to enter into the faith of Christ because that faith was by all its laws super-national; the words of St. Paul concerning the Jews are terrible; their great crime was that they did not want the heathen to be saved:

> For you, brethren, are become followers of the churches of God which are in Judea, in Christ Jesus: for you also have suffered the same things from your own countrymen, even as they have from the Jews: who both killed the Lord Jesus and the prophets, and have persecuted us, and please not God, and are adversaries to all men; prohibiting us to speak to the Gentiles, that they may be saved, to fill up their sins always: for the wrath of God is come upon them to the end (1 Thess 2:14-16).

If it were the business of the Church exclusively to foster a nation's greatness, even if it were of a spiritual order, how could the eight beatitudes survive? they are truly incompatible with any greatness except that of the kingdom of heaven. It is in the fierce conflicts between the Church and racialism, between the Church and nationalism, that we see the demarcations between the human spirit, that is self, and the Holy Ghost who came down from heaven to take men up to heaven.

For the instruction of the reader I ought to remark that the mystery of Pentecost is not directly the mystery of the seven gifts; those seven gifts were always present from the beginning of the world in every soul that was in the state of grace. Pentecost, to make use of a metaphor previously pressed into service, was a new and supremely efficient playing of the Spirit on the seven gifts that were already in the souls of the disciples. In the Pentecostal coming the Holy Ghost produced, through the well-prepared instruments, through the vessels of election, effects of divine harmony such as had never before been heard in the supernatural world here on earth.

✠ 16 ✠

THE RANGE OF THE SPIRIT

THE RELATIVE WORTH OF SPIRITUAL GIFTS IS ONE OF THE most ancient and also one of the most permanent problems that have provoked the interest of Christian thinkers and mystics. We know of the great controversies which existed in St. Paul's days and which engaged the attention of the Apostle in his first Epistle to the Corinthians: "Be zealous for the better gifts. And I show unto you yet a more excellent way" (1 Cor 12:31). "Follow after charity. Be zealous for spiritual gifts: but rather that you may prophesy" (1 Cor 14:1).

Here we are concerned for the moment with the position of those seven gifts of the Holy Ghost of which we have spoken in the preceding chapter: what is their place in the spiritual organism of the Church, and of individual Christians? Are they entirely above the ordinary graces and virtues or are they part of the common spiritual outfit of all those who are in the state of grace? When we speak of the seven gifts of the Holy Ghost we imply by this expression that personal action of the Holy Spirit working on the gifts, as has been already described; so the theological consideration comes back to this:

are Christian souls, through the gift of the Spirit, led to heights of supernatural life for which there is no prescribed form, so that there is no telling what a soul may become under the influence of the Spirit?

At first sight it would seem that the very nature of the Spirit postulates this unreserved liberty of action. Is not this very freedom the one characteristic of the Spirit which Christ singles out?

> The Spirit breatheth where he will, and thou hearest his voice: but thou knowest not whence he cometh and whither he goeth. So is every one that is born of the Spirit (John 3:8).

This view of the Spirit's range of power is, of course, alluring; it implies that above the ordinary Christianity there is the higher Christianity, the Christianity of the mystics, whose only law is the Spirit. But even a superficial examination of the Spirit's work as it is made known to us by the Scriptures, reveals the fact that the chart of the Spirit is something definite, though it may be unlimited in its outlines. The office of the Spirit as delineated by our Lord is a very definite office:

> But the Paraclete, the Holy Ghost, whom the Father will send in my name, he will teach you all things and bring all things to your mind, whatsoever I shall have said to you (John 14:26).

> For he shall not speak of himself: but what things soever he shall hear, he shall speak. And the things that are to come, he shall show you. He shall glorify me: because he shall receive of mine and shall show it to you (John 16:13-14).

There is no misreading the significance of these words: the Spirit is to carry out a well prepared and definite program; He is to make the disciples into spirituals, not through an unlimited exhilaration of mind, but through the manifestation of a light which is more like a beam than an all-round radiation. If now we watch the early Christians at Pentecost and after, we cannot help being struck by the regularity of the manifestations of the Spirit. One might almost say of the Spirit that He is the minister of Christ. He never goes beyond Christ, beyond the mystery of Christ; in the hours of the supremest exaltation, the death and the glory of Christ are the only topics on the lips of the Apostles.

It is, of course, a vital matter for us to know whether the gift of the Spirit is or is not essentially Christological; whether the coming of the Spirit is only the completion of the Incarnation, a completion indeed of infinite magnificence, but still nothing more than a completion. For if the gift of the Spirit were not essentially a completion of the Incarnation, but an addition to it, almost an independent manifestation of God, the consequences of this for the spiritual life of future Christians would be incalculable, and mystical life would vary *toto coelo*, "by the whole breadth of heaven," as we took either the one or the other of these two possibilities.

Now what does the history of the Church disclose to us after the apostolic ages? Has the Spirit in the hundreds of years that have succeeded the first Pentecost led the Church into entirely new regions, into spheres that were not known in the early centuries; or has not the work of the Spirit rather been this, that with a divine sameness He has glorified Christ and manifested Him to all generations, not in a new light, but in the old light unceasingly renewed?

In dealing with this most interesting question, which sums up so much of the Bride's life, we ought to ask for the guidance of Catholic theology in its best and highest form. It is to be admitted that it is not clear to all minds, even amongst theologians, what the range of the Spirit really is. All Catholic theologians would say with one voice that, wherever the Spirit may lead the Church or the individual soul, He never leads them into any form of thought and life and love which would be, even in the smallest way, in opposition to the great fundamental vitalities of Christian sanctity. The three theological virtues of faith, hope, and charity are those fundamental vitalities; at no time will the Spirit raise a man to a region where the writ of those three great powers would not run; St. Paul gives us this assurance:

> Wherefore, I give you to understand that no man, speaking by the Spirit of God, saith Anathema to Jesus. And no man can say The Lord Jesus, but by the Holy Ghost (1 Cor 12:3).

This wonderful ruling of St. Paul makes it certain that the Holy Ghost is always Christological. This is admitted by the universality of Catholic doctors. But with this admission it is still possible to hold that that special action, the coming of the Holy Ghost with the seven gifts, may go beyond the range, not only of the ordinary virtues, but even of the three theological virtues; so that truly, in the power of the Holy Ghost, men may be lifted to heights so great that there is no measuring those heights by any known standards.

The other view is this: that the supreme realities of the spiritual life are precisely those vitalities, the three theological virtues of faith, hope, and charity; and that the Spirit is sent in order to give those three vitalities the fullest expansion possible; that there is no phenomenon in orthodox Christian sanctity, in orthodox Christian mysticism, which is not directly a function of one of these three theological qualities under the breath of the Paraclete. This is the attitude of St. Thomas Aquinas, and this I propose to my reader as being the most perfect concept of the mutual relationship of the Spirit and the Bride.

The three theological virtues have been the object of the speculation and meditation of all Christian generations. They form a sphere of ethics quite unknown to pagan philosophy. They are called theological virtues because it is their exclusive privilege to deal directly with God as He is in Himself: through faith we approach divine veracity; through hope we come into contact with divine fidelity; through charity we are brought face to face with divine goodness. We believe God, we trust God, we love God immediately, in Himself, in virtue of His own personal perfections. Whatever we believe, we hold it because God has said it; whatever we do to save our souls and to arrive at eternal life, we rest our action on God's help which He has promised us; if we love anything or anybody, we do so because we see God in whatever is the object of our affection. The theological virtues are qualities that are in the soul and that enable man thus to lay his hand on God Himself, in belief, in trust, in friendship.

Man cannot come nearer to God than he does in "these three," *tria haec*, whilst he is here on earth. In heaven there will be no faith and no hope, because there will be the clear vision and the unchallenged possession. Charity, however, goes on forever, and it is one of the golden axioms of Catholic theology that substantially the charity of heaven and the charity of earth are identical: "Charity never falleth away" (1 Cor 13:8). For this reason charity is also the greatest of all virtues.

We may put it thus: both subjectively and objectively man has his supremest sanctification through the three theological virtues, through them he is raised almost infinitely above his natural condition. The Bride, the Catholic Church, is constituted through the activity of those three powers.

Let us say that the supernatural Christian world is this: the three planets of faith, hope, and charity. The Holy Ghost, in order to remain within our metaphor, would be the fiery sun. Greater faith, greater hope, and greater charity would be that each planet should receive more of the light and the warmth of the sun, and that all the differences of life and vegetation would come from this, that the planet should incline more or less to the direct influence of the sun, just as in nature we say that the difference between tropical life and the glacial state is not a difference of distance from the sun but a variety of angle. In other words, and perhaps more simply, though I think the comparison helpful, it is the office of the sevenfold Spirit to throw His light and heat on the three virtues, the three planets of the supernatural heaven: faith, hope, and charity. The Spirit is said to do this, and this exclusively; not to create a new faith, but to give faith various degrees of luxuriance of life; not to produce in man a new hope, but to give his hope a certainty which will make it heroic courage; not to bring about a new bond of friendship between God and man other than charity, but to give to charity a sweetness that will make it a foretaste of heaven.

The three theological virtues—and here my cosmological comparison is found useful—are powers that float in the space between heaven and earth. One might almost say they are stern powers, rugged powers, unadorned powers; they are just the powers that establish equilibrium between man and Divinity. Now it is the office of the sevenfold Spirit to clothe with life and verdure the surface of those planets, to make them into Edens, to fill them with every beauty and comeliness, to create the eternal spring. The planets could exist, could have their motions, without all that vesture of beauty and grace; but what a difference there would be! So it is the paramount service of the Spirit that in one way or another He makes of faith, hope, and charity experimental states of the supernatural, giving them a taste which will render man supremely happy here on earth in the possession of those great powers, as if he were in a garden of delights. For we must remember that the three virtues, being so supremely spiritual, are, through themselves, entirely beyond man's feelings and experimentations; they are on the very summit of our rational being, in the cold atmosphere proper to mountain tops.

Through the Holy Ghost we are made to feel, we are made to taste, we are made to enjoy the sublime things of God. So the Holy Ghost may be truly called the God of the Christian experience, and whatever metaphor can represent the happy things of life is appropriate to the Holy Ghost, He is the breath of spring, He is the unction of the mind, He is the comforting voice, He is the gladness of heart. He makes us believe with vision; He makes us hope with the feeling a child has when its hand is held in the warm palm of a strong man; He makes us love, not only with resolve and detachment, but with unspeakable tenderness of heart. This is the work of the Holy Ghost, and all the glorious marvels of experimental Christian sanctity may thus be viewed and explained.

St. Thomas Aquinas, whose description of the role of the Spirit we follow here, starts with the assumption that the three theological virtues, on account of their very perfection, are in a way alien to our nature; they are not rooted in it as are natural powers and instincts. Man has not with regard to them that facility in use which he possesses with regard to his more native endowments. One might say even that there is a kind of awkwardness in all of us in our handling of those most excellent weapons of the highest life. The Spirit then comes to remove all such inhibition, all such awkwardness; He makes the theological virtues more and more congenital to us.

This is the same idea, from another angle; it simply means this, that the Holy Ghost makes the theological virtues into pleasurable operations of the whole man; through the Holy Ghost our mind and our flesh exult in the living God. It is a fact that we ought to remember that the Apostles with Mary the Mother of Christ and all the other disciples were in a state of great purity in preparation for the coming of the Spirit; they certainly possessed the supernatural life in no common degree; they were endowed with faith, hope, and charity; we should have called them holy and so they were. Yet the coming of the Spirit was a new life; not new in the sense of a new revelation, of a new hope, of a new relationship with God, but in the sense of an immense expansion of what was in them, and above all, of a profound experience of all they believed and hoped and loved; an experience that transformed their whole being.

It is ever so in the history of Christian sanctity; the faithful follower of Christ will be lifted to great heights by the Spirit and it will seem to him that all things are new, though on examination he will find that he never disbelieved before what seems to him now so clear and convincing; a new hope has succeeded, not to despair but to mere hesitation; and the All-beautiful shows His face, which was near all along but covered as it were with a mist. This then is the complete operation of the Spirit, both external and internal. It is of course evident that the Pentecostal coming of the Spirit under which we live to this very day, is an internal grace as much as an external sign; but both internally and externally it is essentially an experience. In this it differs from what is called, in strict theological language, the internal mission of the Holy Ghost, which is not the Pentecostal mission but which is a permanent phenomenon of the supernatural order, as we have already said in the chapter on the everlasting Spirit.

✠ 17 ✠

THE SEVEN GIFTS OF THE SPIRIT AT WORK

MUCH HAS BEEN WRITTEN BY CATHOLIC THEOLOGIANS on the seven gifts of the Holy Ghost and their operations in the Christian souls. Of their existence we have a double guarantee: first, they were the qualities that made glorious the soul of Christ. The immortal passage of the prophet Isaiah is, of course, the one classical authority in this sublime matter:

> And there shall come forth a rod out of the root of Jesse: and a flower shall rise up out of his root. And the spirit of the Lord shall rest upon him: the spirit of wisdom and of understanding, the spirit of counsel and of fortitude, the spirit of knowledge and of godliness. And he shall be filled with the spirit of the fear of the Lord. He shall not judge according to the sight of the eyes, nor reprove according to the hearing of the ears (Isa 11:1-3).

The sevenfold power is described again in the last book of the Scriptures under the metaphor of seven horns and seven eyes which belong to the Lamb:

And I saw: and behold in the midst of the throne and of the four
living creatures, and in the midst of the ancients, a Lamb standing, as it were slain, having seven horns and seven eyes: which are
the seven Spirits of God, sent forth into all the earth (Rev 5:6).

Our second authority is the uninterrupted tradition of the
Church, which speaks of those seven gifts as belonging to the Christian soul. We may remind the reader of what we have already said,
that the seven gifts are permanent qualities; they are to be found in
every soul in the state of grace; they are not directly Pentecostal; the
Holy Ghost makes use of those gifts in order to move and elevate the
soul. Since Pentecost, the divine Spirit makes a more abundant use of
them and above all employs them for the purpose of building up the
heavenly Jerusalem, the Catholic Church; in other words, the gifts of
the Holy Ghost have since Pentecost the supreme mission of uniting
all souls into one supernatural Body under the Headship of Christ.
Faith, hope, and charity have become since Pentecost the faith of the
Church, the hope of the Body of Christ, the unity of all the members
in one Spirit; and the seven gifts minister to the theological virtues,
thus enlarged and elevated by the New Testament grace.

It has always been felt by Christian souls that in the activities of
the seven gifts we possess a glorious mysticism which is exclusive to
the Church of God; that a Christian saint is a mystic through the
operation of one or more of those gifts and through nothing else.

The most exact definition of the purpose of those gifts is this: they
deal immediately with Divinity itself in conjunction with the three
theological virtues, but their operations have always something of the
experimental; they create a foretaste of the Godhead which the theological virtues themselves do not necessarily produce. In fact there is

nothing known to us in the natural or supernatural order which could in any way approximate to that sphere of spirituality where the three theological virtues are illumined and vivified by the seven stars of the gifts.

It was to be expected that theologians would try to describe each gift as a separate entity, classifying that most divine reality and showing its difference from the other gifts. It is certain that the seven names stand for seven differences, though it might be permitted to say that they are seven aspects of one and the same divine quality. The gifts do not overlap, but on the other hand, it would be useless to isolate them from each other as if they were seven unrelated individuals in the spiritual order. Distinctions in these high matters never mean separations; they really mean a plentitude of life. It could not be pretended that Catholic theologians are unanimous on every point of their speculations on those gifts; one theologian may speak of one gift as being the source of some high spiritual result whilst another theologian would quote another gift as being the source of that enviable state in the soul. Unanimity in this matter need not be expected and those varieties of opinions in no wise cast any doubt on the reality of the gifts themselves, whose existence seems to belong to the depositum fidei.

The more simple speculations on these matters are truly the more helpful. Our spiritual outfit is like a casket full of precious stones; there are those who would like to know the quality and origin of each stone separately; there are also those who are satisfied with the general impression of beauty and harmony, and we range ourselves amongst them. St. Thomas Aquinas has been content with general principles and he has thus succeeded in creating a definite impression concerning the supreme excellence of the seven gifts. We shall follow him in the brief description of each gift.

To begin with the gift of understanding, *Donum intellectus*. It is a quality that ministers to the theological virtue of faith. Through the virtue of faith the mind of the believer accepts revealed truth, but through the gift of understanding the believer becomes almost a seer; the objects of the faith, which by nature are dark and unseen, all at once acquire brilliancy, they grow almost visible. It is the happy condition of innumerable Christians to whom their faith is an unceasing source of joy; they are at home in it as children are at home in their father's garden. Through that gift the Christian understands the value of the whole supernatural life; he has a practical estimation of all the elements of Christian sanctity; through it man most readily makes of the highest supernatural principles his constant code of action. In one word, through the gift man's intellect turns this way and that way, soars to great heights and descends to the details of human life, with the mobility of the Spirit Himself. The gift of understanding is this: "That the intellect of man should be readily moved about by the Holy Ghost," *Intellecutus hominis est bene mobilis a Spiritu Sancto* (*Summa* II-II, q. 8, a. 5).

Thus is realized the promise of St. John, "You have the unction from the Holy One and know all things" (1 John 2:20). There is no mental ecstasy so sublime in the life of the Christian mystics as not to be covered by the range of this gift. What more could we desire than this condition expressed by Aquinas, man's intelligence offering no obstacle to the Holy Ghost to carry it whithersoever the Spirit wishes to take it?

The gift of knowledge, *Donum scientiae*, also belongs to the intelligence. It is, in the words of the Angelic Doctor, "a certain participated resemblance" of the Holy Ghost: *Quaedam participata similitudo* (II-II, q. 9, a.1, ad 1). The gift is also an adjunct of faith; it enables man to distinguish error from truth in the high spheres of the faith. It is not enough for us to relish the glories of our faith, for there are the powers of darkness, the spirits of error, and through the gift of knowledge we have the divine flair as to what is truth and what is heresy. This gift then is a divine uprightness of judgment in matters of faith, "saving us from mixing the false and the true": *Discernendo scilicet credenda a non credenda* (II-II, q. 9, a. 1).

Through this gift the people of saints are rendered immune from the infection of error which poisons mankind; they escape the snares of the great deceiver, Satan, who seduces all the nations of the earth. This directness of perception of what is true and what is false is, of course, a very evident characteristic of the Catholic Church.

The gift of wisdom, *Donum sapientiae*, is, of all, the greatest gift, if one may make comparisons in divine things. It is more directly connected with charity. It is essentially the gift of the contemplative; in order to describe it St. Thomas uses the words *compassio* and *connaturalitas ad res divinas*, "sympathy" and "natural relationship with divine things," because through that gift charity becomes an experimental tasting of Divinity. That profoundly hidden thing—the state of grace—through the gift of wisdom enters in some way into the conscious life of man, so that he sees and tastes how sweet God is. Here we approach a subject to which there are no other limits than the powers of the Spirit; all the wonderful intimacies of God with man, all the mystical nuptials of the saints, all the woundings of their hearts through the arrow of divine love, are truly the operations of the gift of wisdom. In the ancient phrase of the great mystic, the Pseudo-Dionysius: "Man suffers from God," suffers from the nearness of the divine love; his heart melts under the great fire of God's familiarity. The theological virtue of charity alone could not produce such effect as it is a hidden and unconscious turning of the spirit of man towards God, the final Goal of all things.

The gift of the fear of God, *Donum timoris*, is made by St. Thomas to minister to the virtue of hope. It is the chaste fear which makes us revere God as a father and which above all makes us dread, as the greatest of all evils, lest we depart from Him. St. Thomas sees this connection between hope and the gift of fear that through fear "we dread lest we relinquish the helping hand of God and therefore filial fear and hope are linked together and they complete each other" (II-II, q. 19, a. 9, ad 1). This divine fear, then, may be considered as creating in the Church and in her members that peculiar temperament which is quite unknown to the world, even to the so-called moral world— the fear of losing God, the fear of doing anything which may bring about an estrangement between God and the soul; it makes comprehensible that invocation of the Church: "From thy anger, O Lord, deliver us." It banishes from Christian life every vestige of presumption, of self-sufficiency, of hypocrisy; it is the mother of Christian humility, that wonderful blending of confidence and trepidation in the presence of God.

The gift of counsel, *Donum consilii*, might truly be called the most interesting of the gifts; through it the Church in her administration, individual Christians in their decisions, follow instincts which are beyond all that human prudence can do. Through it, according to St. Thomas, man is "like one who is counseled by God Himself": *Quasi consilio a Deo accepto* (II-II, q. 52, a. 1, ad 1). Rightly in this answer St. Thomas alludes to the uncertainty of all human previsions and to the all-comprehending foreknowledge of God, quoting from the Book of wisdom:

For who among men is he that can know the counsel of God? Or who can think what the will of God is? For the thoughts of mortal men are fearful, and our counsels uncertain (Wis 9:13-14).

Through the gift of counsel the Christian enters into the secret ways of God; unknowingly yet unerringly he will choose, in the practical contingencies of the spiritual life, ways that will lead to eternal salvation. Who does not see what a role this gift must play in the great life of the Catholic Church where decisions are being taken constantly in matters that affect the spiritual welfare of millions?

The gift of fortitude, *Donum fortitudinis*, is more easily understood: its very name shows its purpose. St. Thomas accepts the worth of the natural and the supernatural gifts of fortitude which enable men to do much and suffer much, to undertake great works; then he adds:

But beyond that, the mind of man is moved by the Holy Ghost to this effect that he should bring to a happy conclusion every work which he has undertaken and that he should escape every one of the perils that threatened him. Now to do this is far beyond human nature; for very often it is not given to man to lead to consummation the work he has undertaken or to avoid the evils and perils that beset him as, frequently, he is crushed by them and finds in them his death. Now this is the work of the Holy Ghost in man, that He leads him to eternal life which is the end of all good works and which is the escape from all perils. Of this happy consummation the Holy Ghost pours into man's mind a certain expectation, driving out the contrary fear; and it is in this sense that fortitude is a gift of the Holy Ghost: for it has been said that the gifts represent the motion of the soul through the Holy Ghost (II-II, q. 139, a. 1).

We can readily see what this means for the faith and for the Church; it is the courage of heaven; it is the fortitude of the angels of God; it is the temperament of the warrior of Christ; it gives the Church the courage to attack evil however powerful and however widespread; ordinary human bravery would never suffice for the work which the Church has to do.

The gift of piety, *Donum pietatis*, is thus described by Aquinas:

> The gifts of the Holy Ghost are certain habitual dispositions of the soul through which it becomes promptly mobile under the Holy Spirit. Amongst other things the Holy Ghost moves us to this, that we should have a certain filial affection towards God according to what is written in Romans 8:15: "You have received the Spirit of the adoption of sons in which we cry *Abba* Father"; and as it belongs properly to piety to show God dutifulness and cult it follows that piety, inasmuch as it exercises cult and service to God as to a father through the inspiration of the Spirit, is a gift of the Holy Ghost (II-II, q. 121, a. 1).

The Angelic Doctor completes his thought by saying that it is a portion of the same gift to honor the saints, not to contradict Scripture whether we understand it or not, and to be helpful to those who suffer. He ends with the beautiful remark that through this gift, in heaven the saints shall mutually honor each other, whilst before the Day of Judgment the saints in heaven have pity on those who are still living in this miserable world amongst the tribulations of life. For it is the opinion of St. Thomas with regard to every one of the gifts that they continue in the glorified state; this is why he wants to assure his reader that the saints who are already in heaven have a full scope for that gift because they can have pity on us here on earth.

The reader will perceive readily that infinitely more could be said on this subject. Theologians have worked out with great acumen the effects of these gifts on the Church as a whole and on individual souls; but truly in order to gauge their full bearing in the kingdom of God one ought to write the history of Christian sanctity, a task evidently beyond the power of any man or any group of men. But unless we are willing to read the history of the Church in the light of the seven gifts we renounce the right to speak at all on that subject. The Holy Ghost is the Captain of the army of God; the great war against evil is going on under His leadership, and if we are unwilling to trust implicitly the Spirit who is all wisdom we are liable to make egregious mistakes in our reading of the events and vicissitudes of that great conflict.

✠ 18 ✠

The Powers of the Bride

It is certain that the Apostles considered themselves completely equipped for the mighty task of establishing the Church through the gifts of the Spirit; the whole tenor of the Gospel assumes that one day the Twelve would possess all power to found the kingdom of God. The few words which Christ spoke in the days of His glorification between Easter and the ascension are also redolent of the same emphasis. A power that will be entirely self-sufficient and self-contained will be sent forth into the world. Nothing is more evident in the Acts of the Apostles than this conviction of the early Church that she has power enough to bring about the new order of things; that she needs not to depend on purely natural resources, on the assistance of this world, for her great work. The Church that is born at Pentecost is born in the full vigor of life; she comes forth completely armed with the armor of the Spirit.

The Holy Ghost is not only strength but He is actually an executive power, an element of energy, a force that is partly latent and partly manifest; it is as a manifest force that He is first seen; but His latent energies are also accepted as most solemn realities from the very start. The remission of sins, which is of course a hidden transformation, is attributed to Him. Externally, to the eye, things happen that are only explainable in the supposition that divine energy is at work. All these effects the Spirit produces through the instrumentality of the Apostles and the disciples, that is to say, through the Church. Signs and wonders are multiplied, the Spirit becomes palpable in the marvellous *charismata* of the Church.

From the very beginning we see this difference between fundamental sanctity and powers that are meant to be at the service of that sanctity. There is a vast range of the manifestations of the Spirit which are directly unto utility, in the words of St. Paul; it is their purpose to serve in the establishment of the Church's fundamental sanctity and also, though in a secondary way, in enlarging the Church's sphere of action, in converting men and in bringing fresh disciples to Christ.

I say purposely that the powers of the Church have the propagation of her faith as their secondary object, by which expression I do not mean anything that would belittle this mighty mission of the Church; but it is always necessary for us to bear in mind that all the powers of the Church are meant directly for the Church herself; and for the outside world they are only as an overflow from the Church. It is thus that the Bride is fully arrayed to meet the world, because primarily in herself, for the fostering and protection of her own life, she is well-nigh omnipotent.

The early history of the Church's powers is well known and easily traceable; the Acts of the Apostles and the Epistles are redundant with the subject; the Spirit is seen at work everywhere and in every possible way. Omitting now the latent energies which are identified with the sacramental powers, let us consider the resources the Church had to build herself up into a glorious temple of God.

The theology of the *charismata*, "charisms," of the early Church is a very wonderful province of Christian doctrine. Those powers of the Spirit are essentially, as the Spirit Himself, the token that Christ is in the glory of the Father, as the Victor over all adversity who makes endless largesses on the day of His triumph. The description of that ever ascending energy of the Church, leading to the consummation of the perfect charity, must be given in the words of St. Paul himself:

One body and one Spirit: as you are called in one hope of your calling. One Lord, one faith, one baptism. One God and Father of all, who is above all, and through all, and in us all. But to every one of us is given grace, according to the measure of the giving of Christ. Wherefore he saith: Ascending on high, he led captivity captive: he gave gifts to men. Now that he ascended, what is it, but because he also descended first into the lower parts of the earth? He that descended is the same also that ascended above all the heavens: that he might fill all things. And he gave some apostles, and some prophets, and other some evangelists, and other some pastors and doctors: for the perfecting of the saints, for the work of the ministry, for the edifying of the body of Christ: Until we all meet into the unity of faith and of the knowledge of the Son of God, unto a perfect man, unto the measure of the age of the fullness of Christ. That henceforth we be no more children, tossed to and fro and carried about with every wind of doctrine, by the wickedness of men, by cunning craftiness by which they lie in wait to deceive. But doing the truth in charity, we may in all things grow up in him who is the head, even Christ: From whom the whole body, being compacted and fitly joined together, by what every joint supplieth, according to the operation in the measure of every part, maketh increase of the body, unto the edifying of itself in charity (Eph 4:4-16).

The reading of this glorious passage brings it home to us how the powers of the Church are primarily meant for herself; they are for the profit of the faithful; the children of the Church are protected from the winds of every doctrine, from the cunning craftiness of those that lie in wait to deceive.

Coming now to that well-known and official enumeration of the *charismata* which again is St. Paul's contribution, in his first Epistle to the Corinthians we find the same characteristics. The diversities of graces are manifestations of the Spirit; they are given unto every man to profit, but the man who benefits by them is principally, without any doubt, the believer himself. For those powers are like the members of one body, and that body is the living organism of the Church. The infidel has no part in them and it is only indirectly that he will have the benefit of those marvels when he witnesses the operations of the Spirit: they are not essentially meant to convince him, but to edify the Church. Here again the words of the sacred text must be quoted in their entirety:

> Now there are diversities of graces, but the same Spirit. And there are diversities of ministries, but the same Lord. And there are diversities of operations, but the same God, who worketh all in all. And the manifestation of the Spirit is given to every man unto profit. To one indeed, by the Spirit, is given the word of wisdom: and to another, the word of knowledge, according to the same Spirit: To another, faith in the same spirit: to another, the grace of healing in one Spirit: to another, the working

of miracles: to another, prophecy: to another, the discerning of spirits: to another, diverse kinds of tongues: to another, interpretation of speeches. But all these things, one and the same Spirit worketh, dividing to everyone according as he will. For as the body is one and hath many members; and all the members of the body, whereas they are many, yet are one body: so also is Christ (1 Cor 12:4-12).

The way in which St. Paul makes the infidel a beneficiary is interesting. It is, so to speak, quite by chance and accidentally that the unbeliever finds faith through those gifts; for St. Paul describes the Christian assembly as being in a state of ecstasy, full of divine light, only caring for its own life. It is then that the unlearned Christian or the infidel, as through an accident, comes into the Christian assembly and falls under the spell of the grace:

If therefore the whole church come together into one place, and all speak with tongues, and there come in unlearned persons or infidels, will they not say that you are mad? But if all prophesy, and there come in one that believeth not or an unlearned person, he is convinced of all: he is judged of all. The secrets of his heart are made manifest. And so, falling down on his face, he will adore God, affirming that God is among you indeed (1 Cor 14:23-25).

There is another rendering of the same subject in St. Paul's Epistle to the Romans, where again all the powers of the Church are for the Church herself:

For as in one body we have many members, but all the members have not the same office, so we, being many, are one body in Christ: and every one members one of another; and having different gifts, according to the grace that is given us, either prophecy, to be used according to the rule of faith; or ministry, in ministering; or he that teacheth in doctrine; he that exhorteth, in exhorting; he that giveth, with simplicity; he that ruleth, with carefulness; he that showeth mercy, with cheerfulness (Rom 12:4-8).

The Church, then, without any doubt, has endless resources through which she can survive all the adverse influences of the world, and those powers are hers everlastingly. Their measure may differ according to periods; for they are essentially the result of the vigilance of the Spirit, who gives to everyone according to his need and who bestows talents on every century according to the necessities of the time. But of one thing let us be convinced: the life of the Church is independent of this world, and the Church lives and rules as the mistress of souls in virtue of qualities that are entirely her own. The time of the *charismata* did not end with the apostolic age; they belong, on the contrary, to the very essence of the Church as they are the manifestation of the Spirit. The Church is a society; she is a kingdom, and all her ruling, all her social unification is carried out, not through natural gifts but through the *charismata*. She is the society of the Spirit and even then when she wisely and prudently utilizes human resources, her doing so is in the wisdom of the Spirit, in the *charisma* of ruling.

This is a point on which many do not see clearly. It is evident, of course, that right through the centuries the Church is helped by the natural wealth—material, intellectual, and moral—which is in this world. Often the impression is created that exclusively human elements have a great part in furthering the prosperity of the Church; that men of learning are precious, nay indispensable defenders of the

Church's rights; that the good will of governments is an invaluable asset to the Church's safety; that even material wealth greatly enhances the splendor of the faith. We cannot deny the role of such elements in augmenting the Church's life; they are given to the Church by God's providence as external assets; but none of those things will be of any use to the Church's own life unless she handles them with a talent no one else possesses. By themselves natural advantages can add nothing to the power of the Church; but utilized by her they become the helpers of grace.

What then are the powers of the Church to expand, to convert the unbeliever, to persuade the contradictor? It is, of course, evident that the Church is meant to preach Christ unto all men. Now has the Church a direct *charisma* for that outside work? If so, will it be a *charisma* in a different sense from the *charismata* of the apostolic literature? A *charisma*, properly so-called, supposes faith in Christ, supposes membership with the Body of Christ. Even when it influences and converts the unbeliever it does so because he is the witness of what happens to the person of the believer. The spiritual spectacle of which the Christian is the center makes the impression on the infidel. What then is the power that makes the missionary the propagator of the faith of Christ? It is a power of the highest order, but it is a power that may fail in its effect: the missionary may preach and not be listened to, whilst the *charisma* of the Church is part of her life and therefore always fruitful. In other words, the power that builds up the Church in herself is different in some ways from the power that brings new converts to the Church, on account of the differences in the recipients.

The gift of miracles is the one manifestation of God's presence that is meant more directly for the confirmation of the faith:

But they going forth preached everywhere: the Lord working withal, and confirming the word with signs that followed (Mark 16:20).

To the gift of miracles St. Thomas Aquinas attributes a double function. Firstly and principally it is the evidence of the truth that is being taught. Secondly, it is a proof of the presence of God in man through the grace of the Holy Spirit. The text recalled by St. Thomas is "He therefore who giveth to you the Spirit and worketh miracles among you" (Gal 3:5).

Though the gift of miracles has to be considered as the principal weapon of aggression against unbelief, it is intimately connected with the Church's interior life, as most miracles are wrought inside the Church for the benefit of those that have faith already, although the work of conversion be different. There is, however, no clear line of demarcation between the powers of the Church that build up the Body of Christ and the powers that propagate the Church. One and the same Spirit operates in both directions. Through that same Spirit the Apostles are holy in themselves and powerful as "witnesses of Christ":

> You shall receive the power of the Holy Ghost coming upon you, and you shall be witnesses unto me in Jerusalem, and in all Judea and Samaria, and even to the uttermost part of the earth (Acts 1:8).

There is in the Church this mysterious feature which we might call a biological feature in the supernatural order: all conversions are an adding of numbers to the existing Church and all the power that converts proceeds from the existing Church. The first great conversion is described in such terms, people were added to a society that was there in fullness of life, the preaching of Peter at Pentecost had this result:

> They therefore that received his word were baptized: and there were added in that day about three thousand souls (Acts 2:41).

Through baptism those three thousand also became the Church, and the gift of the Holy Ghost was theirs likewise, for such is the supernatural procedure described by Peter himself on that same occasion:

> Now when they had heard these things, they had compunction in their heart and said to Peter and to the rest of the apostles: what shall we do, men and brethren? But Peter said to them: Do penance: and be baptized every one of you in the name of Jesus Christ, for the remission of your sins. And you shall receive the gift of the Holy Ghost (Acts 2:37-38).

The gift of the Holy Ghost, with all that it means, is the privilege of everyone who is in the Church. Those chosen ones who received the Holy Ghost in the upper room with Mary, the Mother of Jesus, were in an exceptional condition. They had been gathered together by Christ Himself, they had received the faith in His divine Sonship; not flesh and blood had revealed it to them but the Father who is in heaven; they had been the witnesses of all that had happened to the Lord; they were the prepared vessels; they were not in need of conversion any more: they had believed. Between them and Christ there was a link of life which no one else possessed. The Apostles had eaten of His Flesh and had drunk of His Blood at the Last Supper; they had all received the baptism of Christ. No group of human beings ever has been or ever will be in a like condition. Christ speaks of His work in gathering them and keeping them together as of the great success of His life, with the one failure:

> I have manifested thy name to the men whom thou hast given me out of the world. Thine they were: and to me thou gavest them. And they have kept thy word. Now they have known that all things which thou hast given me are from thee: Because the words which thou gavest me, I have given to them. And they have received them and have known in very deed that I came out from thee: and they have believed that thou didst send me. I pray for them. I pray not for the world, but for them whom thou hast given me: because they are thine. And all my things are thine, and thine are mine: and I am glorified in them. And now I am not in the world, and these are in the world, and I come to thee. Holy Father, keep them in thy name whom thou hast given me: that they may be one, as we also are. While I was with them, I kept them in thy name. Those whom thou gavest me have I kept: and none of them is lost, but the son of perdition, that the scripture may be fulfilled. And now I come to thee: and these things I speak in the world, that they may have my joy filled in themselves (John 17:6-13).

When the Spirit came on them, He came to a living organism, not to dead souls; it was truly the application on a magnificent scale of the law of life enunciated by Christ: "For he that hath to him shall be given and he shall abound" (Matt 25:29). Their career in the Spirit started not in death but in life, not in poverty but in wealth, not in darkness but in light; they were not the enemies of God but the dear friends of Christ: "I do not call you servants, but I call you friends" (John 15:15), the Master had said to them only recently.

When the Spirit descended upon them, to crown all the other elections and privileges they became the Church of Christ, one might almost say quite naturally without there being a passage from death unto life. No other men will ever be in the same condition. Those few chosen ones had been grafted on a life that itself is eternal life: the life that came from God when the Word was made Flesh.

Everything, then, in the history of the Church ultimately comes back to something infinitely positive, something immensely actual, something entirely luminous: the life that is in the Incarnate God. The twelve Apostles were in that life in company with her who had given birth to the Son of God. A few more were added to that life, namely those who walked with Christ till He was taken away and who went to the upper room, overflowing with faith and love and intent on the prayer of Christ. The Church's progress through time and space can never be more than this: an addition to that primitive assembly. The way in which these additions are made constitutes the apostolate of the Church; it is something different from her own life, yet something mysteriously connected with that life, for the Church would have neither the will nor the means of gaining new souls unless she were rich in charity and grace within herself.

At no time, however, could Christian apostolate be anything else than a communication of the grace that is in the Church, of the life that is already strong; otherwise the Church's activity would be mere proselytism, an effort to subjugate instead of a communication of charity.

✠ 19 ✠

The Bride and the Sacraments

I**T WOULD BE QUITE INACCURATE TO MAINTAIN THAT THE** concept of the Church was jettisoned at the Reformation; wherever there is any Christianity the idea of a Church is a foremost religious element. It is not the idea of a Church that found disfavor with the Reformers, it is the Church in its concrete form that they fell foul of; the visible, manifest and administrative Church became the butt of their invectives. So the whole anti-Catholic movement has been this: to leave to the Church as few external signs of power and supremacy as could possibly be reconciled with Scriptural language and even to distort the Scriptures in order to get rid of the outward properties of the Church. The invisible Church, the Church of the elect, the Church of the saints, the Church of the spirit, the Church in any form except the Catholic form of undivided and undiminished authority, has gained favor in the eyes of many: this is Protestantism: it is the unwillingness to accept a visible form of human administration as a divine institution and the reluctance to predicate of the historic Church all those glorious privileges which the Scriptures attribute to the Church.

It is, on the whole, a comprehensible aberration, for if the Church could be at the same time real and invisible there would be no scandal, because the power of the Church would not be felt; her claims would not be resented, the signs of her excellence would not be in need of proof, and above all, the sins of her members would not be a stumbling block. For it is the meaning of an invisible Church that only those constitute the Church who are pure before God, who are elect, who are predestined. The Reformers, as we know, defined the membership of the Church in accordance with their various views on man's justification and election.

The Catholic position, then, is this: directly and immediately from the very beginning the Church is made up of mortal men and her powers have visible signs, so that it is known to all men when those powers are active and when they are not active. It has been the burden of this book to show how a visible Church can claim, without pride and without illusion, those sublime titles which Christ and His Apostles have given to the Church. In this chapter we shall consider the spiritualness of those external elements which make the Church more directly into the visible Church, we mean the sacraments and the juridical powers of the Bride of Christ.

The theology of the sacraments and the theology of the Holy Ghost are inseparable. Through the sacraments more than through any other cause the Church is the Bride of Christ:

> Christ loved the church and delivered himself up for it: that he might sanctify it, cleansing it by the laver of water in the word of life (Eph 5:25-26).

These words are allusions to the two fundamental sacraments, baptism and confirmation; baptism, that initiates the soul into Christ and the second sacrament that is an initiation into the Spirit. The waters of baptism prepare for the Spirit, I mean for the Pentecostal Spirit. Every Christian through baptism is in that state in which the hundred and twenty disciples were on the morning of Pentecost, before the third hour of the day, ready vessels, full of spiritual glories but not yet sealed with the Spirit, that special Spirit which was the promise of the Father.

The foundation, then, of the Christian life is the double perfection of the sacrament of the water—or the sacrament of faith as it is called sometimes—and the sacrament of the Spirit:

> In whom you also, after you had heard the word of truth (the gospel of your salvation), in whom also believing, you were signed with the holy Spirit of promise. Who is the pledge of our inheritance, unto the redemption of acquisition, unto the praise of his glory (Eph 1:13-14).

There is only one exception known in this order of succession, the sacrament of water and the sacrament of the Spirit, but an exception so striking that it filled with amazement St. Peter who was the witness of it. Whilst the Apostle was still speaking to Cornelius and his household and was announcing to them Jesus Christ "the Holy Ghost fell on all them that heard the word" (Act 10:44). The Spirit manifested Himself in the same way as He had done at Pentecost: "For they heard them speaking with tongues and magnifying God" (Acts 10:46). This was for Peter a divine indication that the exclusive privilege of the believer—that of being baptized—could not be denied to them:

Then Peter answered: Can any man forbid water, that these should not be baptized, who have received the Holy Ghost, as well as we? And he commanded them to be baptized in the name of the Lord Jesus Christ (Acts 10:47-48).

It is, in truth, an extremely pregnant expression of the lips of Peter, "Can any man forbid water?" The sacramental water is indeed not to be given to any man unless he believe wholeheartedly. On a former occasion in the history of the early Church this is made very clear. Philip the deacon, led by the Spirit, had joined himself to the chariot of the eunuch and had evangelized the man from Ethiopia:

And as they went on their way, they came to a certain water. And the eunuch said: See, here is water: what doth hinder me from being baptized? And Philip said: If thou believest with all thy heart, thou mayest. And he answering, said: I believe that Jesus Christ is the Son of God. And he commanded the chariot to stand still. And they went down into the water, both Philip and the eunuch. And he baptized him (Acts 8:36-38).

Faith, and faith alone, entitled a man to baptism, but the Spirit, who in the case of Philip and the eunuch led the soul of a man to baptism, in the case of Cornelius actually descended in a Pentecostal way on the catechumens before baptism.

The ordinary course, the normal course, has always been this: first the water, then the Spirit:

And it came to pass, while Apollo was at Corinth, that Paul, having passed through the upper coasts, came to Ephesus and found certain disciples. And he said to them: Have you received the Holy Ghost since ye believed? But they said to him: we have not so much as heard whether there be a Holy Ghost. And he said: In what then were you baptized? Who said: In John's baptism. Then Paul said: John baptized the people with the baptism of penance, saying: That they should believe in him who was to come after him, that is to say, in Jesus. Having heard these things, they were baptized in the name of the Lord Jesus. And when Paul had imposed his hands on them, the Holy Ghost came upon them: and they spoke with tongues and prophesied (Acts 19:1-6).

We give this long extract in order to show how, in Christian tradition, there is an intimate association between the water and the Spirit, the sacrament of baptism and the sacrament of confirmation. Through these external acts of the Church men are born to Christ and to the Holy Ghost. The other sacraments may be considered as the full developments of those two profound initiations into the Godhead through which men are made the members of Christ and are sealed with the Spirit of promise. Quite truly these sacraments are considered to constitute the Christian's fitness for all the other marvels of the kingdom of Christ and for all the other operations of the Spirit.

The more we associate our sacramental theology with the theology of the Pentecostal Spirit, the nearer we shall be to a perfect understanding of those marvellous means of grace which are so entirely the property of the New Testament Church; the Holy Ghost is everywhere in the working of the sacraments; and though at first sight there might seem to be an opposition of character between the Spirit and the material thing, in reality the material sign is the means preferred by the Holy Ghost for His operations as well as for His manifestations. As He showed Himself at Pentecost under external signs, so likewise He operates in the Church under the visible elements of the sacramental order.

It is a complete misunderstanding of the Spirit to consider palpable and visible realities as being an obstacle to His advent. This false spiritualness has, as we know, worked great havoc in Christendom since the days of the Reformers. On the other hand, we have to avoid the error of divesting the sacraments of the Spirit; it is the Holy Ghost who operates in them, and sacramental life is wonderfully fertile, is inexpressibly beautiful precisely owing to that all-enveloping activity.

The far-reaching conclusions of Catholic theology concerning the efficacy and the causation of sacraments could surprise those only who do not habitually associate the sacraments with the Holy Ghost nor recognize that through the presence of the Spirit each sacrament is linked up, through all space and all times, with the cause of all sacramental grace—the death of Christ on the Cross. Sacraments are also sources of special graces which are certainly a portion of the Pentecostal dispensation, graces not known before Pentecost. From these graces is born the social order of the New Testament, the union of all Christians in one Body, Christ.

Now it is the Spirit who has, so to speak, the special mission of vivifying the Body of Christ. In the Eucharistic mystery the Spirit, by appropriation at least, is invoked as the power that will bring about the great presence of Christ: "Come, thou who makest holy, almighty and everlasting God" (*Canon of the Mass*). The *sanctificator*, "sanctifier," is, of course, the Spirit, the Holy Ghost.

The remission of sins is through the power of Christ's resurrection; it was communicated to the Apostles through Christ's breath when, as the Victor over death, He came back in triumph:

> Now when it was late that same day, the first of the week, and
> the doors were shut, where the disciples were gathered together,
> for fear of the Jews, Jesus came and stood in the midst and said
> to them: Peace be to you. And when he had said this, he showed
> them his hands and his side. The disciples therefore were glad,
> when they saw the Lord. He said therefore to them again: Peace
> be to you. As the Father hath sent me, I also send you. When he
> had said this, He breathed on them; and he said to them: Re-
> ceive ye the Holy Ghost, whose sins you shall forgive, they are
> forgiven them: and whose sins you shall retain, they are retained
> (John 20:19-21).

The powers given by the sacrament of Holy Order are all powers
of the Spirit, as such powers were not exercised before Pentecost. The
words of Simon Magus as narrated in the Acts are illuminating in the
extreme, though they be words expressing the sin of simony: "Give
me also this power, that on whomsoever I shall lay my hands, he may
receive the Holy Ghost" (Acts 8:19). We know Peter's answer:

> Keep thy money to thyself, to perish with thee: because thou
> hast thought that the gift of God may be purchased with money.
> Thou hast no part nor lot in this matter. For thy heart is not right
> in the sight of God. Do penance therefore for this thy wicked-
> ness: and pray to God, that perhaps this thought of thy heart
> may be forgiven thee. For I see thou art in the gall of bitterness
> and in the bonds of iniquity (Acts 8:20-23).

The Church in her Ordinal, from the ordination of the *ostiarius*,
"doorman," up to the episcopal consecration, abounds in the con-

sciousness of the role of the Spirit in creating the Christian hierarchy. The Catholic priesthood is truly the gift of the Spirit.

As a gift of the Spirit we must envisage what St. Thomas calls the most material of all the sacraments, Christian matrimony. We have to come back over and over again to St. Paul's Epistle to the Ephesians; the great sacrament in Christ and in the Church—matrimony—has been for ever spiritualized through this, that it is expressive of Christ's union with His Church, of Christ's death on the Cross when His side was opened and there came forth Blood and water. The Spirit of sanctification is the Spirit of the Bride; therefore it is the Spirit of Christian matrimony. Christian matrimony as a sacrament is directly Pentecostal because it is the natural foundation of the supernatural society which was founded at Pentecost.

In the Spirit the Christian who is sick receives comfort and refreshment; through the presence of the Spirit he knows himself to be a branch on the tree of life; for even in death the Spirit rules supreme, as He is the Spirit of resurrection.

As it would be a sad mistake if we detached the theology of the sacraments from the mystery of Pentecost, so it would be a grave error if the power of administration which is in the Church were not constantly idealized through the Spirit. It is perhaps the one manifestation of the Church's life here on earth which meets with least sympathy from the modern mind; the power of ruling seems so unspiritual, it has all the air of being a mere imitation of the ways of the world, of powers that claim no spirituality. Is there any difference, it is asked, between Papal imperialism and the domination of any secular dynasties?

To this there is at once the answer that all ecclesiastical power has for its object the oneness of the Church. How, we ask, has this oneness been obtained, how has it become a visible reality? There can be but one answer to this query: the Catholic Church is one because she is the Body of Christ. Her oneness is her evident sign amongst all nations; it is a unity of faith as well as a unity of obedience.

Now is such a result possible outside the sphere of the Holy Ghost? There have been many attempts to unite men into some social or national entity; we know how miserably they have failed. So we might take it for granted that, even if externally the administrative life of the Church seems not to differ from other administrations, internally, in reality, there is a principle of oneness for which the world looks in vain. We know the classical phrase in which the decisions of the Church's administrative power are couched: "It hath seemed good to the Holy Ghost and to us" (Acts 15:28). The ordinances of the ruling powers of the Church have this character: the Holy Ghost and the Church constitute one authority. And through the oneness of these two powers there is preserved the oneness of the Church which is the most evident spiritual marvel here on earth.

✠ 20 ✠

IN SINU ECCLESIAE

THE EUCHARISTIC MYSTERY IS AN INTEGRAL PORTION OF the mystery of the Church. Some may find it strange to hear it said that so divine an institution as the Eucharist is a portion of another institution, the Church. The meaning of the phrase is this: the Eucharist is essentially and intrinsically united with the life of the Church; it is, in fact, comprehensible only through the Church. It is, to use an ancient expression, *in sinu Ecclesiae*, "in the bosom of the Church." At no time and in no wise is the Eucharist outside the Church. The Church on her side with regard to it, is not in the attitude of one who worships something extraneous, something superimposed upon her life, something that is high up in the sphere of the supernatural, far beyond the Church's own region. But the mystery of the Body and the Blood of Christ is in the bosom of the Church herself, there it takes place, as the Incarnation took place in the bosom of the immaculate Virgin.

What we might call the "immanence of the Eucharist within the Church" is an aspect very often lost sight of, much to the detriment of Catholic theology. The Eucharist is not a heavenly mystery; it is directly an ecclesiastical mystery; by its very essence it belongs to the state of the Church as she is on this earth. This we express when we say that the Eucharist is a sacrament. Like the other sacraments, the limits of its functions are conterminous with the limits of the Church who walks by faith, who dwells in this world. The results of the mystery are to be found primarily in the Church militant; its ministers are those whom the Church ordains, its rights are ecclesiastical rights, its life mixes with the stream of sanctity that is still on trial; it is not in the heavenly consummation, but prepares for man the heavenly consummation. The best analogy for this embosoming of the Eucharist in the Church would be, as already insinuated, the nine month's life of the word Incarnate in the virginal womb of the Mother of God.

When, therefore, the Church celebrates the Eucharistic mysteries she does not stretch forth to the unseen regions of heaven; she is not laying hold on a distant Bridegroom; she sends forth no piercing cry to call Him down from the skies: on the contrary, she enters into herself, she utters words of power, a power that resides within herself. She becomes conscious of a presence that was there potentially all the time; she speaks phrases and performs actions that are more like the monologues of a person full of joy than conversations with an outsider, with a stranger. She herself, in the words of the Council of Trent, offers up the Eucharistic sacrifice, and she offers it up with the divine Gifts which she herself has put there on the altar in virtue of the sacramental energy that is in her.

It is, of course, beyond all doubt that the Christ who is in the Eucharistic mystery is a different Person from any human person or from any aggregate of human persons, however holy; but it is also a fact, which our faith guarantees, that this Eucharistic Christ is in the

Church through the sacramental act of the Church in the words of the Consecration, and through no other act. The Son of God places Himself in the very bosom of the Church in that great mystery, not through an independent deed of His, but through the sacramental act of the Church. He is not like a guest who comes and goes; He is more like a child whom the Church takes into her arms and holds with every kind of affection and fondles as she wishes. What is called sometimes, rather incorrectly, the "mystery of Christ's obedience in the Eucharist" is this very thing, Christ's profound identification of Himself with the Church's sacramental power. It would be more true to say that He is born in the Church than to say that He obeys the Church when He renders Himself Eucharistically present.

If we visualize the Eucharistic mystery as a profound identification of the Son of God with His Church—always, of course, keeping in mind the diversity of personality—it will be easy for us to find an explanation for the Church's Eucharistic behavior; for we may indeed speak of Eucharistic behavior with regard to the Church. What man, however illumined, could have written for the Church a code of conduct in this matter? Taking for granted the data of the faith, the Real Presence, who would have been capable of prescribing for the Church the true manners of treating such a Presence? How is the Bride to behave when thus brought into a terrifyingly near contact with supreme majesty? A thousand solutions are possible, at least hypothetically, ranging from deepest awe to utmost familiarity.

The Church's own solution may be expressed in the words of the Canticle of Canticles: *Dilectus meus mihi et ego illi*, "My Beloved belongs to me and I unto Him" (Cant 6:3). The Church makes her Eucharistic Lord part of her own life. He is truly as much subjective as objective: the Eucharistic immolation is so completely interwoven with the

Church's rite that it is not possible to separate them in practice. There is not one moment precisely defined and set apart as the sacrosanct point of time when the Eucharistic immolation may be said to stand clear and isolated from all human acts of religion, when the Son of God, in His own Person, by an act unmistakably distinguishable, offers Himself on the Christian altar: He is not appearing for one blessed second, to disappear again the moment He has done the great deed of Eucharistic immolation. Such is not the manner of the Eucharistic sacrifice. On the contrary, with great freedom and amplitude of speech, with many rites and ceremonies, with prayers and invocations the Church offers up the sacrifice, holding in her hands for a considerable time the divine Elements of the immolation, speaking words of praise, making commemorations of the living and of the dead, superimposing her own life on the divine Victim, keeping that Victim in her heart and speaking to God as if she herself were the high priest and victim. For the great act of supreme worship, the sacrifice, is done in an entirely human way, with preparation, with reiteration of rites, with the climax of the act, to be followed by new protestations of loyalty to God, the supreme Lord of all things, by thanksgiving for gifts received.

Such behavior would not be legitimate unless this complete identification of Christ and His Church in the Eucharistic mystery be taken for granted. If Christ were one agent and the Church another agent, the Christian canons of the sacrifice would be meaningless; if the two realities, the Spouse and the Bride were kept severely apart it would not be possible for the Christian liturgy to follow the developments it has done. The principal development has been this: that the consecrated Elements are kept by the Church close to her heart in a movement of prayer and intercession that may be prolonged indefinitely. It is as if the Church herself were in a Eucharistic state and spoke to the Father from the depths of the Eucharistic mystery. The partaking by the faithful of the Body of Christ has no other law than this one: that the recipient should be in the charity of Christ.

We know, of course, that there are certain disciplinary laws of the Church, the principal one of which is that the faithful do not partake more than once a day. But this is merely disciplinary; the Eucharist itself is not bound by any limitations; the freedom of the faithful to eat this Bread and to drink this Cup is truly unlimited. The precept given to the Christians by Christ is couched in the most generic terms: they must eat His Flesh and drink His Blood. That supersubstantial food has, in a way, the "commonness" of all food; it is found everywhere, it can be eaten by everyone who has life. If it is described by Christ as a food that comes down from heaven this description by no means conveys rarity or distance: it is not a food that only a few of the elect are fortunate enough to seize upon in its mysterious descent from heaven. Christ, on the contrary, by that very expression, "the food that comes down from heaven" (John 6:33, 50) means to convey its "commonness," for it is an allusion to the manna, that miraculous food which covered the ground every morning and could be picked up by the hands of men and women and children in the measure they liked.

The Church has a gift of understanding that enables her to deal with the Eucharist thus profusely; she is truly the "Bethlehem," the House of the divine Bread. When she is fed Eucharistically she is not like the prophet, retired in deep solitude, far from all enemies, receiving food miraculously through the ministrations of a raven. Her feeding, on the contrary, is like the repast of the five thousand, who were satiated and who, after having eaten their fill, could still behold the baskets holding a superabundance of the same food. In the Eucharistic Banquet the Church behaves with an astonishing normalness, one might almost say with a complete absence of wonder, as if the divine Bread were of her own making. This familiarity with the heavenly Bread is indeed a truer behavior, one more completely in accordance with the character of that mystery than would be an attitude of awe and surprise, as those are awed and surprised to whom something unusual happens, something miraculous. The heavenly Bread is certainly *in sinu Ecclesiae*, "in the bosom of the Church."

The abiding presence of Christ in the Eucharist—what is called in sweet modern phraseology, the "Mystery of the Tabernacle"—is not a new mystery, but a further instance of the Church's power to hold her Eucharistic Lord enshrined in her own life. In exact theological thought the reservation or preservation of the consecrated Elements, after the consummation of the sacrifice, is no new marvel, it is part of the mystery of the heavenly food. The Eucharistic existence of Christ is above time and space, and the element of duration, as such, adds nothing to the principal mystery.

But there is on the part of the Church a new grace, a new understanding; she knows how to make use, in time and space, of a secret that transcends both time and space. In her own life she actually approaches the hidden God under the sacramental veils in a completely human manner, and gives to her devotion and her love the external adjuncts of terrestrial life. She dwells with her Bridegroom for hours and for days; she watches over Him and with Him; she counts her mystical communication with Him in time divisions as every other human deed is measured by the movements of the clock; she speaks of "perpetual adoration," she speaks of "day and night adoration," she speaks of solemn adorations lasting "forty hours," with a complete realism, as if her timeless Lord had entered into her existence, had made

Himself subject to the limitations of her own time-divided life.

We shall never possess a satisfactory theology of the Eucharist unless we give great preponderance to the Church's Eucharistic character, to the Church's marvellous capacity of responding, in her own life, to all the aspects of that mystery in which her Spouse has chosen to approach her. It is not enough for the Church to have faith in the Eucharist; she has her own Eucharistic instincts. There is in her a psychology which comes from the Spirit and which is completely attuned to the great sacrament of love. It would then be most exact language to say that the Eucharist is in the Church, that the Church keeps it, nurses it almost as a mother nurses her child, protects it, gives it a home here on earth. Christ is truly in the midst of His Church through the Eucharist; He has innumerable contacts with the souls whom He has redeemed, and from sunrise to sunset without ceasing there goes on that palpitating double life, the life of Christ in the sacrament and the life of the Church through the sacrament.

It is the sense of the whole liturgy of the Eucharist that the Church offers herself to God in union with the divine Victim, Christ. The traditional rite which embodies this fellowship of oblation with Christ is the mixing of water with the wine; the drop of water signifies the union of the Church with her Spouse in the divine oblation. Moreover the gifts of bread and wine are particularly expressive of this same mystery; Christians are supposed, in principle, to bring their own bread and wine, that bread and wine which presently will be transubstantiated into the Body and the Blood of the Son of God:

> This our offering, do thou, O God, vouchsafe in all things
> to bless, consecrate, approve, make reasonable and acceptable
> (*Canon of the Mass*).

Nothing could bring home more forcibly the special feature of the Eucharistic mystery, that it is indeed part of the Church's life, than this prayer of the Canon; in the Eucharist more than anywhere else it becomes manifest that, in the words of St. Paul, Christ cherishes and nourishes the Church as His own Flesh.

✠ 21 ✠

The Spirit, the Bride, and the World

I T IS IMPOSSIBLE TO BE OCCUPIED WITH THE MATTER OF this book on the Holy Ghost and the Church without being brought up very soon against the formidable fact of the apparent disproportion between believers and unbelievers, between those in whom the Spirit dwells and those who to all appearances are entirely outside the influences of the Spirit, between the power of the Church and the power of the world.

This problem is so insistent and so vexatious that it may be said to spoil the happiness of the Catholic theologian. On the one hand he is the champion of a divine institution; on the other, he cannot be blind to a reality which is as vast as the world, the disproportion of which we have just spoken. Though this matter enters into practically every aspect of the Church's doctrine and is never far from any tractate of the theology of the Church, it behooves us to treat it *ex professo*, "avowedly," and to speak more amply of the problem.

We could wish, of course, that we had been given by Christ a clear pronouncement as to what He meant His Church to be in this world.

Thanks be to God, we possess all we could possibly wish concerning that other problem, the life of the Church considered in herself; of it more than we can understand has been told us by Christ and by the Apostles. This present book is chiefly concerned with the Church in herself, as the reader may easily see, if he has followed us so far. But we have no such clear utterances on the other point, on what we might call the place of the Church in the world and the proportion in number and earthly power between the Church and mankind in general.

One fact however is certain and it is this: at no time does Christ commit Himself to the promise that His Church and mankind will be conterminous, that all men sooner or later, will enter the Church and remain in it permanently. Not only does He send His Apostles like lambs among wolves—this was inevitable as the initial condition of their apostolate, for the Church was born in the midst of a world that had fallen away from God—but there is no hint on the part of Christ that this condition will be altered in the course of centuries. In all He says about the Church's position in this world, He seems to lay down principles of conduct that suppose a permanent hostility on a large scale between the world and the Church. When He tells the Apostles that in this world they shall be straitened, He takes, as He so often does, the apostolic group as being representative of the whole future:

> If the world hate you, know ye that it hath hated me before you. If you had been of the world, the world would love its own: but because you are not of the world, but I have chosen you out of the world, therefore the world hateth you. Remember my word that I said to you: The servant is not greater than his master. If

they have persecuted me, they will also persecute you. If they have kept my word, they will keep yours also (John 5:18-19).

Even a superficial study of the other documents of the New Testament will bring home to us the fact that at no time did the Apostles expect any other future than one of combat and temptation; they seem to be full of the conviction that the number of disciples that had come to Christ through their ministry constituted that victory which had been promised. The indifference of the rest of the world did not appear to affect them; their own work had been successful. On the other hand, it is also evident that Christ meant the Gospel to be preached to all men, and the zeal of the Apostles knew no limits; but from the very beginning the great enterprise is presented to us as one where failures will be as numerous as successes:

Go ye into the whole world and preach the Gospel to every creature. He that believeth and is baptized shall be saved: but he that believeth not shall be condemned (Mark 16:15-16).

One fact is certain, however, and this is the very essence of the Gospel, that the unbelief of others in no wise debars the believer from the full enjoyment of the whole mystery of Christ as contained in the Church. To him the kingdom of God has come in all its power and he is not expecting anything else; he is not waiting for the conversion of the world in order to give thanks for the surpassing grace of Jesus Christ.

We may, therefore, consider the Church to be thus constituted according to Christ's intentions: at every moment of her existence she is the kingdom of God, fully, completely, unreservedly, with all the powers of the Spirit at her disposal; she is queen over the world through her very excellence, even if untold millions of men be provoked to contradiction and hatred by the fact of her presence. It is evidently thus that Christ willed His Church to be situated. He has not revealed to us how ultimately, when all things will be judged and brought to light, the souls of men will have been affected by the Church's presence; but He has given us enough indications concerning the nature of that presence to make us realize that the Church is essentially a shining light in a dark world and a power that shall be contradicted.

From that Church, virtue will go out into the world and many there will be who will be brought from death to life, whom the Church will raise up and take to her bosom and give them also the life that is in her:

> You are the salt of the earth. But if the salt lose its savor, wherewith shall it be salted? It is good for nothing any more but to be cast out and to be trodden on by men. You are the light of the world. A city seated on a mountain cannot be hid. Neither do men light a candle and put it under a bushel, but upon a candlestick, that it may shine to all that are in the house. So let your light shine before men that they may see your good works and glorify your Father who is in heaven (Matt 5:13-16).

More than ever today the minds of fervent believers are agitated with the problem which is now called technically the problem of the "salvation of the infidel." It is obvious from the very way in which the matter is put that it is only the believer, and we may even add, the fervent believer, who formulates the problem; the infidel himself, whosoever may be the man to whom the term applies, is of course the very last person to be worried by the problem; he neither knows

it nor feels it, for it is his very infidelity to have no perplexity about
an ultimate salvation; had he such a perplexity we could hardly call
him an infidel anymore. It is therefore an anxiety which can be felt
by those alone who are safe within the house of the Church. But that
anxiety, as I said, seems to be quite peculiar to our own days and more
than one big volume has been written on this very subject, though
of course we have to admit that there is no kind of revelation on this
matter, no sort of principle which belongs to the *depositum fidei*, except the general assertion that God wishes all men to be saved:

> Who will have all men to be saved and to come to the knowledge
> of the truth. For there is one God: and one mediator of God and
> men, the man Christ Jesus (1 Tim 2:4-5).

Christ only spoke of the Church, the Apostles only knew the Church,
and so we may take it as the only rational position to be adopted by
the Catholic thinker that everything has to resolve itself unto the one
problem of the Church.

It is an *a priori* possibility, which I think we shall all admit, that
God can make provision for the whole of mankind in the supernatural
sphere through one portion of mankind, that portion which is directly and unmistakably sanctified and in which is found the fullness of
grace, the fullness of intercessory power and the fullness of apostolic
efficiency. From this sanctified core of humanity there would proceed
an endless wave of supernatural magnetism which would leave no
one untouched or unenergized. In such a hypothesis, then, whatever
salvation there is in the world at large would be through the Church
directly, so that the presence of the Church in mankind would be the
supreme mercy in store for the human race; not only for the actual
members of the Church, but for the whole family of men.

The mysterious point of interrogation would be this: how much or how little of the influx of that central focus of energy would be necessary in order that any given human individual be in the supernatural state and consequently be endowed with the possibility of salvation? No doubt it will not be possible to settle to our satisfaction a matter which is so entirely the secret of the Spirit; but I do not think that anyone could doubt God's power to leaven the world with supernatural life through a definite institution such as the Church.

It is my opinion, then, that the Catholic Church in actuality holds the position which I have described as a hypothesis. It is certain that even the members of the Church, those who professedly are Catholics, benefit by the Church immensely more than they can be aware of: that power of intercession which is implied in the Eucharistic sacrifice of atonement, even in our own case, is far beyond our conscious contribution to the Church. It will be said, of course, that we are the beneficiaries of those transcending riches of the Church precisely because we have been grafted on the Church through faith and through baptism.

But we must also remember that through the Church directly, much is given to those who are not in charity with God, to those Christians who are in the state of mortal sin. Their case presents at least an analogy with the innumerable human beings who are also in darkness but who have not at any time, consciously, renounced God. This, of course, is the condition of almost the universality of human beings. It is evident that the so-called infidel has no direct dispensation under which he can be saved; there is no revelation for him; there are no sacraments for him; his only chances of salvation are in this, that he should come into the Church, actually, as a converted believer, or unconsciously, as one who is purified through influences whose origin he does not know.

We do not consider that there is any reason to establish a radical difference between the so-called infidel and the non-Catholic Christian in this matter of salvation through the One, Catholic, Apostolic, and Roman Church. It is simply axiomatic in our theology that the Spirit, through the Pentecostal coming, dwells in the one religious society in communion with Peter, He would not be the Spirit of truth if He were the abiding Spirit of two societies professing contradictory creeds. The corruption of doctrine destroys the temple of the Spirit. It is of course happily a fact that most of the non-Catholic Christians have been baptized in Christ, have been sanctified by other sacraments, and are professing positively most of the essential truths of Catholicism. All this means that, everything considered, they are immensely nearer to the influence of the living Body of Christ than is the non-baptized infidel. Still the difference of nearness and remoteness is one of degree, not one of kind. Where there is rejection of one of the truths of the Spirit, there is banishment from the House of the Spirit, and one who acts thus is not in the Church, though he may receive much from the Church, as bread is sent from the house of the bridegroom when the nuptial feast is being celebrated to the many outside.

To establish the Church in every country, not as an unconscious influence, but as a conscious power, is of course Catholic missionary work. Even a small group of Christians in a pagan land will be a force greater than we can imagine, just as the hundred and twenty disciples became a power so great that there never will be the equal of it. It is a debated matter among theologians how much true belief is actually necessary in order to make supernatural justification possible. The two doctrines, of the existence of God and of God's will to reward the good and to punish the wicked, seem to be the minimum, without which no man can be sanctified in his soul. If any human being possesses such a belief, however awkwardly that belief may be expressed, the influx of the central power of the Church becomes a possibility.

This will not mean in practice that the Catholic missionary will not be full of zeal to manifest the full truth of God to all men. A fire must consume everything that is within its reach though its heat may go far beyond the actual sphere of its activity. The Christian apostle will never rest, the charity of Christ presses him, and the Church has an internal power of expansion. Apostolic zeal is, of course, in all instances nothing else than the flame of the Spirit. The apostle wants what the Spirit wants, what Christ wanted, who came to send fire upon earth and who said that His passion was to see it lighted everywhere:

> I am come to cast fire on the earth. And what will I, but that it be kindled (Luke 7:49)?

In this amazing saying Christ makes the very distinction which runs right through the supernatural order, the actual presence of the fire and its expansion. It is indeed wonderful that Christ in His own Person should use this metaphor in order to express the zeal that was in Him—a fire that is to be lighted all over the world. In other words, Christ's supreme will is this: to see His established Church everywhere, for she is the great fire.

We may say that the true formula for Catholic missionary zeal is this: to establish and plant the Church there where the Church has not been before. If we read the Acts of the Apostles carefully we shall certainly gain the impression that apostolic activity was essentially directed to the foundation of churches everywhere, of Christian communities, with the full hierarchy, with the complete working of a spiritual system. The conquest of the individual soul seems to be subordinate to the vaster scheme of establishing the Church; it would be a very incomplete concept of Catholic activity in the mission fields to think only of the salvation of individuals: such is not directly our work as missionaries.

The establishment and the building up of the Church is our work. We know how in practice, through the centuries, the missionary enterprises of the Church have had that characteristic of expanding a spiritual empire from a center, with the whole apparatus of a supernatural administration. The Church progresses as a conquering power, not as one which goes forth to capture individual souls; the salvation of souls is a very definite kind of work, for it is salvation through the Church: let the Church be established and souls will be saved.

✠ 22 ✠

The Riches of the Bride

THE THEOLOGICAL EXPRESSION, THESAURUS ECCLESIAE, "Treasury of the Church," is a household word with Catholics. In the religious controversies of the last four centuries the *Thesaurus Ecclesiae* plays a leading role, as it well might. The metaphor—for a metaphor it is—stands for a reality so deep that no man can fathom it. The outlines of the doctrine of the Church's Treasury are well known. The Church is said to be possessed of a surplus of spiritual values which is actually infinite and therefore inexhaustible. The spiritual values in question are the expiatory or satisfactory works for the remission of the results of sins committed by men. These works are the acts of Christ, the Son of God, and of His saints. At no time are the saints separated from their Head, Christ, when there is mention made of the *Thesaurus Ecclesiae*. Those accumulated values need not lie idle in the sight of God.

The Church, through the Pope to whom all power is given, can grant a share in those riches to any of her children. This is done directly through the use of the sacred Indulgences. As the doctrine of the Indulgences was the starting point of the Protestant heresy it is no wonder that the *Thesaurus Ecclesiae* has been a burning question in the doctrinal feuds of the modern world ever since the Renaissance period.

It is not my purpose to write here a treatise on Indulgences, though the Bride's glory would be much enhanced by the worthy exposition of so holy a subject. I do not think that the concept of the *Thesaurus Ecclesiae* is fully covered by the theology of Indulgences. Most likely Indulgences are only one of the signs of the superabundance of the Church's spiritual wealth. It is my intention here to use the doctrine of the *Thesaurus* as a guide for further investigation into the Church's inward life. Indulgences are a beacon of light revealing the Church's true height, besides being an immense profit to the faithful.

Let us then put the matter thus. A Church that proclaims herself to be possessed of the kind of wealth revealed in the *Thesaurus* doctrine, is a society of such excellence and originality that membership in it must be supremest privilege. Now this is the conclusion that matters here: the resolute acceptance of the unifying work of the Holy Ghost inside the supernatural society, the Church, is the only logical attitude for anyone who believes in the *Thesaurus Ecclesiae* to adopt. The starting point of that faith is the marvellous reality expressed by St. Paul in words of matchless power:

> For as the body is one and hath many members; and all the members of the body, whereas they are many, yet are one body, so also is Christ. For in one Spirit were we all baptized into one body, whether Jews or Gentiles, whether bond or free: and in one Spirit we have all been made to drink (1 Cor 12:12-13).

Now the first consequence of this oneness is this, that no Christian possesses a spiritual life that is isolated and detached from the lives of other Christians. It is true, of course, that everyone who is sanctified in Christ keeps his personality undiminished. Through the use of his free will does the Christian become a saint, does he attain higher sanctity or remain in a lower degree. It is again through independent exercise of his unhampered choice that he practices during life a definite mode of perfection. He is a priest, a religious, a worker, nay even a martyr, by his own election. The oneness of Christ's Body is no obstacle to such individuations of personality and grace. The doctrine of the mystical Body, on the contrary, presupposes the complete rounding off of the human personality.

But there comes the Spirit, whose mission and efficiency is never better manifested than in this very thing, that He makes so many free wills conspire into one action, and the fruits of that action are the common good of the whole society, because by its very nature the action was one in purpose. It is the Spirit who stirs up the wills of men, it is the Spirit who keeps those wills attuned, it is the Spirit who leads them to the perfect act. So one might say that from an *a priori* point of view all the deeds of sanctity in the nearly infinite kingdom of God are common good, because there is only one principal author of them all, the Spirit.

We have to appeal to other doctrines in order to know what in that production of the spiritual wealth belongs to any one person exclusively, so that it cannot be transferable. We say, then, invoking the principles of the theology of merit, that the increase of merit itself is not communicable, because merit is the supernatural stature of every elect. All other spiritual worths and values are transferable. They are not of such a nature as to be attached to one elect more than to another. This is true more particularly of the work of satisfying for sin. It would seem that the one thing that matters is that God shall receive satisfaction for the offences committed against His divine Majesty. This compensation may be forthcoming from any member of the Church. All the other members are bound to be beneficiaries of this moral adjustment, because they are one moral person.

Such views would sound preposterous in any other connection. But if we make that supposition, which is of course the boldest of all hypothetical positions, that all Christian souls are moved by one Spirit, the glorious dream of a supernatural state of undivided privilege becomes a reality.

But we ask ourselves, with bated breath, what must then be the nearness of Christian souls to each other if such a thing can happen? Is it possible for finite spirits thus harmonized not to feel each other's proximity? Who will lift the veil for us, to enable us to gaze at that spectacle of millions and millions of souls moving with the beat of the Spirit?

The communicability of spiritual values amongst the members of the Church is one marvel. The immensity of those values is the second glory. In this matter the Church takes quite a practical attitude and she translates into external administration her internal consciousness. She takes it for granted that the *Thesaurus* is infinite and therefore inexhaustible. The Church's theologians abound in the same sense and the most exact-minded amongst them use terms that convey their conviction that the surplus of satisfactory works is absolutely unlimited in extent.

We must bear in mind that whenever there is a question of this wonderful *Thesaurus* as above said, mention is made of the united worth of Christ and of His saints. Together the divine and the human workers have achieved that great result and are going on achieving it.

That the satisfactions which the Son of God presented to the Deity for the sins of men should be infinite, is comprehensible enough.
But the language of the Church is not only applicable to the infinite
Person of Christ but also to the finite human beings who through
their deeds of sanctity and repentance have made the Church incom-
prehensibly rich:

> Let us be glad and rejoice and give glory to him. For the mar-
> riage of the Lamb is come: and his wife hath prepared herself.
> And it is granted to her that she should clothe herself with fine
> linen, glittering and white. For the fine linen are the justifica-
> tions of saints (Rev 19:7-8).

The Christians of all times, when their works are put together,
will be found to have done not only their share, but more than their
share, to give back to God the glory which the sins of men have di-
verted from Him.

In order to do this matter full justice one ought to give an ex-
haustive treatise on the doctrine of good works, that sweetest of all
the revealed verities which, alas! is the sign over which there arose
the great contradiction, the heresy of the sixteenth century. May one
not entertain a lingering hope that a division of spirits, occasioned by
a misunderstanding of what constitutes a good work, may be more
easily healed than separations of a fiercer kind, as when Christians
differed over the Nature of God?

It is not the aim of this book to enter into a subject so full of
practical application. The Council of Trent has done nothing greater
than its restatement of the traditional faith on justification and good
works. The vision of St. John is an impression which is a sufficient
presentment of this matter. The Bride is worthy to meet the Bride-

groom; it is given to her to appear in a garment of dazzling whiteness. Left to our own imaginings we should have said the garb stands for the "justifications" of the Son of God Himself. The seer was instructed differently. It is the justifications of the saints, therefore of men, that cause the dazzling vision.

It is a peculiar feature of the Church's spiritual wealth to remain unobserved by the eyes of men until the great day of the revelation. The words taken from the Apocalypse of St. John betray this element of surprise at the greatness of the Bride's splendor through the justifications of the saints. The angel that showed John all the marvels overpowered the old Apostle's mind with the brilliancy of the scenes painted:

> And I fell down before his feet, to adore him. And he saith to me: See thou do it not. I am thy fellow servant (Rev 19:10).

There is, to begin with, that universal cause of concealment of the glorious life that is in us, its very excellence. In most of its manifestations supernatural life practiced by man here on earth is not perceptible to any observer:

> Dearly beloved, we are now the sons of God; and it hath not yet appeared what we shall be (1 John 3:2).

Much of the Church's sanctity is visible. It is the purpose of this book to reiterate that supremely important fact. But immensely more remains unseen. The Church has the qualities of the risen Christ. After His victory over death Jesus Christ conversed with men. His resurrection was evident; but no eye could behold the glory that was in Him.

There seems to be, moreover, a direct divine ordinance that the

Church's sanctity should only partially appear to men. Christ keeps His Bride veiled until the hour of the nuptials. Persecutions, temporal misfortunes, the sins of the Church's individual members, are the sackcloth in which the wife of the Lamb sits and mourns as if she were not the Queen she really is.

There is in the Apocalypse the opposition between the Lamb and the Beast: there is also that further contrast, the Bride and the harlot. The passage from the terrible vision ought not to be abbreviated here as it is the embodiment of a mystery which meets us everywhere, the external splendor of the anti-Christian world:

> And he took me away in spirit into the desert. And I saw a woman sitting upon a scarlet colored beast, full of names of blasphemy, having seven heads and ten horns. And the woman was clothed round about with purple and scarlet, and gilt with gold and precious stones and pearls, having a golden cup in her hand, full of the abomination and filthiness of her fornication. And on her forehead a name was written: A mystery: Babylon the Great, the mother of the fornications and the abominations of the earth. And I saw the woman drunk with the blood of the saints and with the blood of the martyrs of Jesus. And I wondered, when I had seen her, with great admiration. And the angel said to me: why dost thou wonder? I will tell thee the mystery of the woman and of the beast which carrieth her, which hath the seven heads and ten horns (Rev 17:3-7).

It is a result of the gift of the fortitude which the Spirit imparts to be thus able to face the reality of evil without blenching. The Christian is one who is endowed with the gift of knowledge, a quality that enables him to see both good and evil with equal clearness. At no time do we give such incontestable evidence of possessing a divinized mind as in this power to gaze undisturbed upon evil. St. John gives us a very full description of the apparel of the scarlet woman while he confines himself to a mere hint at the whiteness of the Bride's garment.

Sin is multitudinous, justice is one. It is therefore one of our most useful endeavors as Catholics to make a profound and persevering study of the hidden sanctities of the Church in the past and in the present. It is an art that must be acquired and can be greatly developed by every one of us. But unless we make at one time of our life a determined mental stand against "official history" we shall never behold that great vision. History practically never presents us with any true account of the Church's spiritual life. We have to discard appearances, we have to go below the surface, we have to fall back on certain realities, so obvious that the historian never mentions them.

One such reality, amongst a thousand others, is this, that the Eucharistic sacrifice has been offered up unceasingly in the Church for nearly twenty centuries. To fix one's eyes on a spectacle of that kind, will soon produce something of that wonderment concerning the Bride's riches that overcame John when he fell down to adore the angel whose hand had lifted a corner of the veil.

✠ 23 ✠

The Brotherhood that is in the World

"BE SOBER AND WATCH: BECAUSE YOUR ADVERSARY THE devil, as a roaring lion, goeth about seeking whom he may devour, whom resist ye, strong in faith: knowing that the same affliction befalls your brothers, who are in the world" (1 Pet 5:8-9).

The episode in the life of Elijah the prophet where utter despondency succeeds an act of supreme courage and faith is dear to many a contemplative. At the prayer of the prophet the fire of the Lord fell from heaven consuming the holocaust on the altar erected on Mount Carmel, so that not only the wood, but even the stones and the dust were devoured by the flames, which finally licked up the water that was in the trench. On the strength of this manifest divine intervention, in strict justice according to the statutes of the theocratic system under which both the worshipper of Jehovah and of Baal lived, the prophet caused four hundred and fifty priests of Baal to be killed in the bed of the torrent Cison.

Both sides had staked their all on this divine manifestation. But Elijah had not reckoned with Jezabel, and from her face he fled because she had uttered a great curse and had asked the gods to treat her abominably "if by this hour tomorrow I make not the life of Elijah as the life of one of them" (1 Kings 19:2). Elijah lost his head:

> And rising up he went whithersoever he had a mind. And he came to Beersheba of Judah, and left his servant there. And he went forward, one day's journey into the desert. And when he was there, and sat under a juniper tree, he requested for his soul that he might die, and said: It is enough for me. Lord, take away my soul; for I am no better than my fathers. And he cast himself down, and slept in the shadow of the juniper tree (1 Kings 19:3-5).

Then came the visit of the angel, the comforting food, the march of forty days and forty nights to the mount of God, Horeb. When finally the Lord comes He asks the prophet the question: "What dost thou here, Elijah" (1 Kings 19:13)? The prophet's answer is a magnificent protestation of zeal on the one hand and a lamentable confession of failure on the other:

> With zeal have I been zealous for the Lord God of Hosts; because the children of Israel have forsaken thy covenant. They have destroyed thy altars; they have slain thy prophets with the sword. And I alone am left: and they seek my life to take it away (1 Kings 19:14).

To this lamentation the Lord replies in a very different tone:

> And the Lord said to him: go, and return on thy way through the desert to Damascus. And when thou art come thither, thou shalt anoint Hazael to be king over Syria. And thou shalt anoint Jehu the son of Nimshi to be king over Israel. And Elisha the son

of Saphat, of Abel Mehola, thou shalt anoint to be prophet in thy room. And it shall come to pass, that whosoever shall escape the sword of Hazael, shall be slain by Jehu: and whosoever shall escape the sword of Jehu, shall be slain by Elisha. And I will leave me seven thousand men in Israel, whose knees have not been bowed before Baal, and every mouth that hath not worshipped him kissing the hands (1 Kings 19:15-18).

The prophet is the pessimist: the Lord is the optimist. If those two terms were ever aptly applied to two simultaneous moods, this was the occasion. Not a word of the long tale of woes that came from the lips of Elijah is repeated by the divine voice. God does not seem to enter into His servant's point of view even one hairsbreadth. The King of heaven gives direct orders that will have incalculable consequences, and those orders are not such as a leader would give to a beaten army to save its retreat. The prophet is sent forward with an entirely new plan of campaign, with a fresh divine policy.

Ahab and Jezabel, the human monsters who had frightened out of his wits that bravest of all men, are not even mentioned; the sword of Jehu, a completely new power, will dispose of them. But above all, the prophet who was but a man had not seen what the eye of the Lord had beheld all along. Under that apparent ruin of the house of God there was life to an unexpected extent: "Seven thousand men in Israel whose knees have not been bowed before Baal." It is not God then—who after all alone is ultimately interested in the spiritual state of mankind—who takes the despondent view, it is the man, the holy man, who has God's glory at heart, it is he who makes those sweeping declarations as to the hopeless state of God's kingdom. The prophet did not know that a new order of things was on the point of being made manifest, that there was an indomitable kernel of loyal believers. God knew all these things and the cause of Jehovah was as safe as ever. Hence the divine optimism.

We are happily not in need of applying to our own days in all its features this thing that happened to Elijah. Great as our losses are, the people who have not kissed the hand of Baal are to be met with everywhere and they are quite clearly in evidence. Satan has no such uncontested, apparent victory as he had in the days of Jezabel; yet the main lesson of the prophet's interview in the cave on Horeb remains. There is present today a great spiritual power that endures undefeated, though much of it is hidden. The Church of our own times is indeed a wonderful spectacle to the eyes of angels and of men. As truly as ever the Church that is in the world is the Body of Christ, the Bride of the Lamb, the House of God, the Pillar and ground of truth.

There can be no doubt as to the high sanctity of vast numbers of those who constitute the Catholic Body all over the world. To single out one fact only, there are innumerable religious Communities in every part of the globe in which spiritual life is at an average as high as it was in the early days of Christianity. There is no aspect of the supernatural order which is not familiar to those who have dedicated their whole life to the service of Christ.

Paul and Barnabas received this testimony from the Apostles in the letter sent to the churches: "Men that have given their lives for the name of our Lord Jesus Christ" (Acts 15:26). Are there not countless men today in the Church to whom this testimony, superb as it is, would be applicable in its full bearings? Is there not visible everywhere a splendid devotion to the interests of Christ, a fine sense of enterprise for the extension of the kingdom of God?

The open attack against Catholicism by Protestantism is now four hundred years old; the attack on Christian faith generally by modern infidelity has lasted nearly two hundred years. Has this stream of poison sullied the Church? Has it been possible for the dragon to swamp her through the very size of the lie and calumny vomited against her?

> And the serpent cast out of his mouth, after the woman, water, as if it were a river: that he might cause her to be carried away by the river (Rev 15:26).

A Church that remains uncontaminated after four hundred years of the river of mental venom is indeed the victorious Bride of Christ. She is the great sign appearing in heaven, "a woman clothed with the sun, and the moon under her feet, and on her head a crown of twelve stars" (Rev 12:1). Who will deny that the One, Catholic, Apostolic and Roman Church has preserved her dogmatic whiteness, her incorruption of faith?

But it will be said there are also the sinners and the load of lukewarm souls. This indeed is a sad fact, but both sin and lukewarmness are rebuked unceasingly by the Church; they are being fought night and day; they are never accepted by her as works of life, as does the modern world, but they are always regarded as works of death. Sin does not pollute the Church, but compromise with sin would do so.

If the Church had no power and no will to react against sin and lukewarmness then would the transgressions of the faithful be a permanent stain on the Church's robe; but is it not a universally received fact that the confessional is the Church's most living institution? When we see our large crowds of simple believers thronging to our churches from all the poisonous atmosphere of modern life, when we see their repentance and humility, are we not justified in applying to those multitudes who come with their sins to Christ's tribunal those words from the Apocalypse:

> Blessed are they that wash their robes in the Blood of the Lamb: that they may have a right to the tree of life and may enter in by the gates into the city (Rev 12:14).

What is the State of the world outside the circle of repentant Christians? Again the words of St. John may be quoted, strong as they are:

> Without are dogs and sorcerers and unchaste and murderers and servers of idols and everyone that loveth and maketh a lie (Rev 22:15).

It is precisely in these matters that the great divide of spirits is to be found, repentance and callousness, keen sense of sin and hardness of heart.

Let us repeat it once more, though the thought has been expressed often in this book: the whiteness which Christ expects from the Church is the whiteness, not only of baptism but also of the justification produced by the sacrament of penance, that second uninterrupted baptism of the Christian people. A moment's thought, a most elementary sense of the proportion of things, ought to bring home to us that we are members of a great people, that the Catholic brotherhood all over the world is truly in ancient language, "the society of the saints":

> You are a chosen generation, a kingly priesthood, a holy nation, a purchased people: that you may declare his virtues, who hath called you out of darkness into his marvelous light: who in time

past were not a people: but are now the people of God; who had not obtained mercy: but now have obtained mercy (1 Pet 2:9-10).

Peter applied these words literally to "the strangers dispersed through Pontus, Dalmatia, Cappodocia, Asia, and Bythinia" (1 Pet 1:1). Could not Peter's successor of today, in all literalness, speak thus of multitudes vastly more dispersed and immensely more numerous than was Peter's flock? To pray with those countless multitudes of souls, to believe with them, to worship with them in the oneness of the sacred liturgy, to suffer and to repent with them, to atone with them, to love with them, in one word, to be united with them in a life that reaches from end to end, because the Spirit is one, is indeed the glory of the Christian brotherhood.

✠ THE END ✠

Scriptural Index

GENERAL INDEX

A

Abel Mehola 187
Abraham 21
Adam 52
ad extra 15
adoration, Eucharistic 165–166
Ahab 187
Alexandria 59
Andrew, St. 19
angels 28, 29, 31, 72, 105, 115–116,
      138, 188
  angelic life 103
  beholding the Spirit 101, 114, 116
  biblical appearances 10, 61
  fall of 117–118
  united by the Spirit 101–103
Apollo 59, 154
apostasy 65
Apostles. *See* disciples
  at Pentecost 19, 23, 102–103
  disciplinary rulings 30
  hated by the world 169–170
  missionary zeal 175–176
  their union with Christ 148–149
apostolate 150, 169
apostolic age 23, 28, 108, 124, 145
apostolic language and literature 10, 25,
      27–28, 111, 146
a priori 7–8, 21, 36, 107, 172, 179
Aquinas, St. Thomas
  on "formed faith" 75, 79
  on gifts of the Holy Ghost 133–139
  on miracles 147
  on theological virtues 125–126, 128
Arabians 12
Arius 113
ascension 2, 9–10, 35, 44–45, 47, 51,
      140
Asia 12, 191

B

Baal 62, 84, 185–188
Babylon 62, 183
baptism
  fundamental sacrament 152–155
  of Christians 65, 142, 148, 173, 190
  of Jesus 16, 20, 23, 35, 52, 54, 148
  of John 35, 46, 54, 58, 105, 155
  of the Spirit 58
Barnabas, St. 188
Bartholomew St. 19
Beast of Revelation 32, 34, 183
beatitudes 119–120
beauty 117, 127, 133
  of faith 75
  of the Church *ii*, 32, 72–73
  of the Holy Spirit 101–103
Becket, St. Thomas 62
Beersheba 186
Belial 31
Bethlehem 10, 13, 35, 164
Blood of the Lamb 33, 66, 190

CPSIA information can be obtained
at www.ICGtesting.com
Printed in the USA
LVHW011156190420
654025LV00014B/1987

9 780615 827810